HOME REPAIR AND IMPROVEMENT

FLOORS AND STAIRWAYS

BY THE EDITORS OF TIME-LIFE BOOKS, ALEXANDRIA, VIRGINIA

The Consultants

William Covey has been active in the floorcovering industry for more than 30 years. He founded the Northern Virginia Floor-covering Association in 1984 and is an active executive board member of the Virginia Floorcovering Association. He owns Covey's Carpet and Drapes, Inc., and is part owner of Technical Flooring Services, both located in Springfield, Virginia.

Jeff Palumbo is a registered journeyman carpenter who has a home-building and remodeling business in northern Virginia. His interest in carpentry was sparked by his grandfather, a master carpenter with more than 50 years' experience. Palumbo teaches in the Fairfax County Adult Education Program.

Mark M. Steele is a professional home inspector in the Washington, D.C., area. He has developed and conducted training programs in home-ownership skills for first-time homeowners. He appears frequently on television and radio as an expert in home repair and consumer topics.

CONTENTS

Restoring Damaged Floors

1

Any flooring from attic to basement needs regular maintenance and occasional repair. Closely linked to the framing of a house, floors often suffer from shifts in the underlying structure. Other enemies are moisture, abuse, and age. Whatever caused the damage, repairs are usually possible. Some, like replacing a joist or girder, are major projects, but most require only a little time—plus the right materials and approach.

WARNING - UNPLUG
POWER CORD BEFORE
REMOVING LAMP GUARD

Quick Cures for Wood Floors

Although durable, wood floors are subject to a variety of ailments—among them, squeaks, bouncing, cracks, stains, and burns. Most maladies can be easily remedied. If the damage is serious, you can replace boards without leaving visible scars.

Problems beneath the Floor: Squeaks are usually caused by subflooring that is no longer firmly attached to the joists or by the rubbing of finish floorboards that have worked loose from the subfloor. Retightening either can be done in a number of ways, explained at right and on page 10.

Squeaks, along with bouncing, may also indicate a lack of bridging—diagonal braces between joists, needed for any joist span of 8 feet or more. If this reinforcement is missing, install prefabricated steel bridging.

Sealing Cracks: Cracks between boards open when humidity and temperature changes cause uneven shrinkage. Plug them with a mixture of sawdust from the floor itself and penetrating sealer. Gather the dust by sanding boards in a corner of a closet. Work 4 parts sawdust and 1 part sealer into a thick paste and trowel it into the crack.

Surface Defects: Stains and burns, if not too deep, can be erased by sanding. To determine the extent of the damage, go over the blemished area with a wood scraper. If the defect starts to lift out, the board can be saved by sanding and refinishing; otherwise, you will have to replace it.

Patching a Damaged Floor: Replacement of ruined boards is best done in the winter, when dry furnace heat will shrink the wood and ease the job of fitting in new pieces. Inspect for decay in the subfloor if you see any sign of rot in the floorboards: With an ice pick or awl, pry up some wood; if it feels spongy or cracks across the grain, rot has set in. Treat lightly decayed subfloors with a preservative containing pentachlorophenol. If the rot has penetrated through the wood, replace the subflooring.

 **TOOLS**

Hammer
Stud finder
Electric drill
Nail set
Screwdriver
Putty knife
Mallet
Wood chisel
Pry bar

 **MATERIALS**

Construction
  adhesive
Finishing nails or
  trim head screws
  (3")
Wood shingles
Screws and washers
Glazier's points
Steel bridging
Replacement
  boards
Flooring nails (3")

 **SAFETY TIPS**

When hammering nails, wear safety goggles to protect your eyes from flying debris.

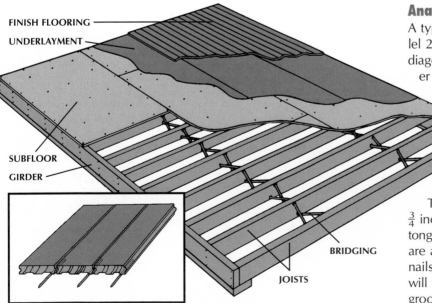

FINISH FLOORING
UNDERLAYMENT
SUBFLOOR
GIRDER
BRIDGING
JOISTS

Anatomy of a wood floor.

A typical wood floor is constructed in layers. Parallel 2- by 8-inch joists, laid on girders and braced by diagonal bridging, provide structural support. In older homes, the subfloor is often wide planks or tongue-and-groove boards laid diagonally for extra stability. Today, sheets of $\frac{3}{4}$-inch plywood are preferred; they are usually glued as well as nailed to the joists. A moistureproof and sound-deadening underlayment of heavy felt or building paper is laid atop the subfloor. The finish flooring, most commonly strips of oak, $\frac{3}{4}$ inch thick and $2\frac{1}{4}$ inches wide, has interlocking tongues and grooves on the sides and ends. They are attached by driving and setting 3-inch flooring nails at an angle above the tongues, where the nails will be concealed by the upper lips of the adjoining grooves *(inset)*.

Shimming the subfloor.

If the subfloor is accessible from below, have someone walk on the floor while you look for movement in the subfloor over a joist. To eliminate movement, apply a bead of construction adhesive to both sides of the tapered edge of a wood shingle and wedge it between the joist and the loose subfloor. Do not force the subfloor upward or you may cause boards in the finish floor to separate.

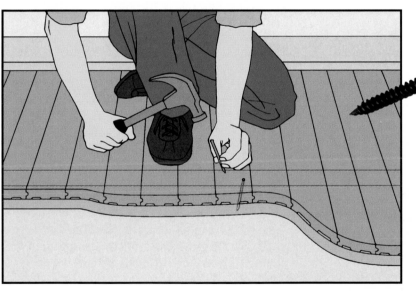

TRIM HEAD SCREW

Securing inaccessible subfloors.

If the ceiling beneath the floor is finished, refasten the loose section of subfloor to the nearest joist through the finish floor above.

◆ Use a stud finder to locate the joist. Then drill pairs of pilot holes angled toward each other and drive 3-inch finishing nails or trim head screws *(photo)* into the subfloor and joist below.

◆ Set the nailheads or countersink the screws and cover them with wood putty that has been tinted to match the color of the boards.

Anchoring floorboards from below.

◆ Select screws that will reach to no more than $\frac{1}{4}$ inch below the surface of the finish floor.

◆ Drill pilot holes through the subfloor, using a bit with a diameter at least as large as that of the screw shanks, so that the screws will turn freely. Avoid penetrating the finish floor by marking the subfloor's thickness on the drill bit with tape.

◆ Drill pilot holes into the finish floor with a bit slightly narrower than the screws.

◆ Fit the screws with large washers, apply a bit of candle wax to the threads to ease installation, and insert them into the pilot holes. As you turn the screws, their threads will bite into the finish floorboards, pulling them tight to the subfloor.

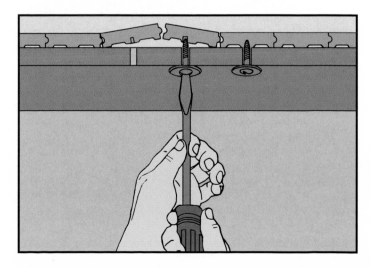

Silencing finish flooring from above.

◆ First, try remedies that do not mar the finished surface. Force powdered graphite or talcum powder into the joints between boards.

◆ If the squeak persists, insert glazier's points—the triangular metal pieces that secure glass into frames—every 6 inches and set them below the surface with a putty knife *(right)*. If the pressure of the knife is insufficient to push the points down, use a hammer and small piece of scrap metal to tap them into place.

◆ Should these solutions fail, drive finishing nails or trim head screws through the floorboards and into the subfloor, angling and concealing them as explained on page 9.

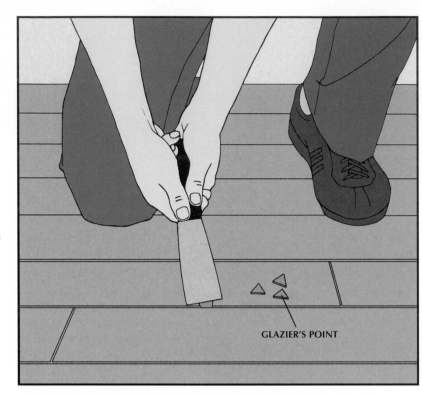

GLAZIER'S POINT

Installing steel bridging.

Prefabricated steel bridging comes in sizes to fit between joists spaced at 12, 16, and 24 inches. To install the braces, hammer the straight-pronged end into a joist near the top. Then pound the L-shaped claw end into the adjacent joist near the bottom. Alternate the crisscross bridging pattern from joist to joist, making sure the pieces do not touch each other.

CUTTING OUT A DAMAGED AREA

1. Making end cuts.

◆ Remove boards in a staggered pattern, with adjacent end joints at least 6 inches apart. At the end of a damaged board, make a vertical cut with a sharp 1-inch wood chisel, keeping its bevel side toward the portion of the board to be removed.

◆ Working back toward the vertical cut, angle the blade and drive the chisel at about 30 degrees *(inset)* along the board.

◆ Repeat this sequence until you have cut all the way through the board. Repeat at the other end.

2. Splitting the board.

◆ With the chisel, make two parallel incisions a little less than an inch apart along the middle of the board from one end to the other.

◆ Use the chisel to pry up the board between the incisions just enough to split the wood.

3. Prying the board out.

◆ Working on a board at the center of the damaged area, insert a pry bar into the lengthwise crack created with the chisel. Pry the middle strip out, then the groove side of the board, and finally the tongue side.

◆ Remove adjacent boards in the same way, working toward the edge of the damaged area and taking care not to harm any good boards. Remove exposed nails or drive them down with a nail set.

◆ Take a sample of the flooring to a lumberyard to get matching replacement boards.

PATCHING THE HOLE

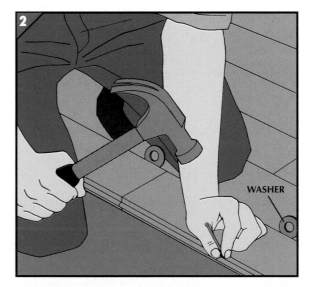

1. Inserting a new board sideways.

Cut a replacement board to fill the outermost space on the tongued side of the damaged area. Using a scrap of flooring with a groove that fits the tongue of the replacement piece as a hammering block, wedge the new board securely into place.

2. Blind-nailing a board.

Drive and set 3-inch flooring nails at a 45-degree angle through the corner of the tongue of the replacement piece. Pilot holes are not essential but may be helpful. If existing boards around the repair have separated slightly, try to match their spacing by inserting thin shims such as metal washers between the new board and the old one while driving the nails.

3. Inserting a new board lengthwise.

To slide a replacement between two boards, lay it flat on the subfloor and work the tips of its tongue and groove into those of the existing pieces. Using a scrap hammering block, tap it all the way in.

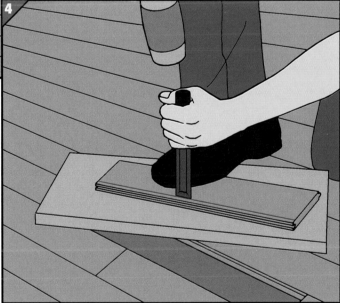

4. Inserting a new board from above.

◆ For the last few spaces where you cannot slide the pieces into place, lay a replacement board upside down on a piece of scrap wood and chisel off the lower lip of the groove as indicated by the blue line on the board at right.
◆ Turn the board faceup and gently tap it into place from above.

5. Face-nailing.

◆ To fasten the last replacement boards, which offer no access for blind-nailing, drill angled pilot holes every 12 inches about $\frac{1}{2}$ inch from the edges of the face. Drive 3-inch finishing nails or trim head screws into the holes.
◆ Set the nails or countersink the screws and cover them with wood putty that has been tinted to match the color of the boards.

A small dip in a floor is irritating but not necessarily dangerous. If less than $\frac{3}{4}$ inch deep and 30 inches long, the dip can be repaired with hardwood wedges driven between a joist and the subfloor *(page 9)*.

A larger sag, in conjunction with other symptoms such as a sticking door, cracked plaster, or leaky plumbing, may indicate structural damage in the supporting framework of joists, girders, and posts.

Pinpointing the Problem: Inspect the framework underneath the floor *(below)* for structural members that are defective. If you have a second-story sag, an entire floor or ceiling may have to be torn out before you can get at the trouble and repair it.

Test for rot and insect damage by stabbing the wood with an awl. Rotted wood feels spongy and does not splinter. A honeycomb of small holes signals termites or carpenter ants; if you find such holes, call an exterminator at once.

A sound joist can be straightened permanently by having a new joist nailed to its side, a technique called doubling *(page 16)*. A slightly rotted joist can also be doubled if it will hold a nail—and if you first coat it liberally with a penetrating wood preservative. Always replace a joist that is thoroughly rotten or insect infested *(pages 17-18)*.

Where a drooping girder is the cause of a sagging floor, the repair may entail the substitution of a

steel column for a wood post *(pages 19-21)*, the installation of a new girder *(pages 22-27)*, or both.

Jacking Up the Floor: In order to make any of these repairs, you'll need to jack up the joists or girder under the sag. The jacking techniques shown here for an unfinished basement also apply to finished areas of the house, once you have exposed the supporting framework of the floor.

Always use a screw jack; the hydraulic type is neither as strong nor as reliable. If you are working in a basement, rent a house jack; in a crawlspace, use a contractor's jack. In either case, grease the jack threads before you begin.

 TOOLS

Straightedge (8')
Telescoping house jack
Contractor's jack

 **MATERIALS**

Pad (4 x 8)
Beam (4 x 6)
Blocks (2 x 6)
Timbers (6 x 6)

 **SAFETY TIPS**

A hard hat guards against painful encounters with joists, girders, and exposed flooring nails.

What holds up a floor.

At the ground floor of a typical house, joists are laid across the shorter dimension of the foundation. Outer joist ends rest on the foundation sills; inner ends rest on a girder supported by posts anchored in concrete footings that may include raised piers. The built-up girder shown here, made of lengths of lumber cut to overlap atop a post, rests in pockets in the foundation wall. Cross members called bridging strengthen the joists and keep them in alignment. Other elements called trimmer joists and headers frame a stairwell opening. Trimmers and headers consist of two boards nailed together to carry the extra weight of the stair and of joists cut short of the foundation sill *(page 76)*.

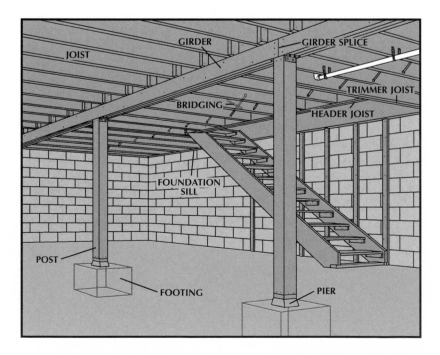

JACKING UP JOISTS

Measuring a sag.
◆ Lay an 8-foot straightedge—either a 2-by-4 or the factory edge trimmed from a sheet of plywood—across the sagging area. Measure the gap between straightedge and floor and mark the floor where the sag is deepest.
◆ Measure from the mark on the floor to two different reference points—walls or stairways, for example—that lie at right angles to each other and that are visible in the basement. There, take measurements from the reference points to position the jack.

STEEL PINS

PAD

PIPE

Jacking from a basement.
◆ Extend the jack to fit between the joist and the floor with about 12 inches to spare, and lock the tube at that length with the steel pins provided.
◆ Set the bottom plate on a length of 4-by-8 lumber. While a helper steadies a 4-by-6 beam at least 4 feet long between the joists and the jack's top plate, screw the jack until the beam presses against the joists. Plumb the jack with a level, then nail the plates to the beam and pad.
◆ Remove the bridging between a joist to be doubled or replaced and its neighbors. To keep the joists parallel, cut 2-by-6 spacers to fit snugly between them and insert as shown on page 16.
◆ Once a day raise the jack no more than $\frac{1}{16}$ inch, about a half-turn. If necessary, slip an 18-inch pipe over the jack handle for leverage. Because the floor will settle after the jacks are removed, raise it $\frac{1}{4}$ inch higher than level.

Jacking from a crawlspace.
◆ Assemble a pyramidal framework, called cribbing, from hardwood 6-by-6 timbers, available from dealers in structural timber. Stack the timbers as shown at right, placing the ones at the top of the structure about 18 inches apart.

◆ Atop the cribbing, set a 4-by-8 pad for the jack, then raise the jack to meet a 4-by-6 beam held across the joists.
◆ Install spacers as described above, then raise the jack $\frac{1}{16}$ inch a day—one-eighth turn on most contractor's jacks—until the floor is $\frac{1}{4}$ inch above level.

Once you have decided whether to double a joist or replace it *(page 14)*, proceed as described on these pages. In either case, electrical cables, pipes, and ventilating ducts that run perpendicular to joists can be substantial hurdles.

Circumventing Obstacles: You can get around one or two such roadblocks when doubling a joist by using the technique shown at the top of the next page. But in some instances of doubling—and often when replacing a joist—it may be more practical to temporarily remove a section of ductwork or to unstaple electrical cables from joists to improve access. When a pipe intrudes, the simplest solution is to notch the joist to fit around it.

One-for-one replacement of an unsalvageable joist is usually suffi-cient. However, if the old joist has sagged badly enough that the sub-floor above it has split or broken, you'll need to install a second new joist for added support.

Choosing Lumber: Buy doublers and replacement joists to match the old joist in every dimension. The single exception is the height of doublers that you plan to use for reinforcing a notched joist. All of the boards should be straight and free of cracks or large knots; if rot has been a problem, use pressure-treated lumber. Before you install a doubler or a new joist, find the crown, an edge with a slightly out-ward, or convex, curve. Install the board with the crown facing up-ward, against the subfloor; the joist will be forced straight by the weight that it bears.

 TOOLS

Floor jack
Plane
Pry bar
Reciprocating saw

Saber saw with flush-cutting blade
Carpenter's nippers
Wood chisel
Cat's paw

 **MATERIALS**

2 x 4s
2 x 6s
Joist lumber
Steel bridging

Construction adhesive
Common nails ($2\frac{1}{2}$" and $3\frac{1}{2}$")
Finishing nails (3")

SAFETY TIPS

Protect your eyes with goggles when hammering or pulling nails, using a hammer and chisel, or sawing wood with a power saw. Add a dust mask when cutting pressure-treated lumber, and wash hands thoroughly after han-dling it. Wear a hard hat when han-dling heavy objects overhead.

DOUBLING A JOIST

Attaching the new joist.
◆ Remove bridging, insert spacing blocks, and jack up the floor *(page 15)*.
◆ Plane a $\frac{1}{4}$-inch-deep, 18-inch-long notch in the new joist's ends *(inset)*. Remove a spacer and test-fit the joist. Deepen the notches as needed.
◆ Lay a bead of construction adhesive on the top edge of the new joist. While a helper holds it tight against both the old one and the subfloor, fas-ten the doubler to the joist with $3\frac{1}{2}$-inch common nails, staggered top and bottom every 12 inches. Hammer the protruding nail points flat.
◆ Trim $1\frac{1}{2}$ inches from the spacer removed earli-er, and toenail it between the doubler and the neighboring joist.
◆ Remove the other spacing block and install new bridging *(page 10)*.

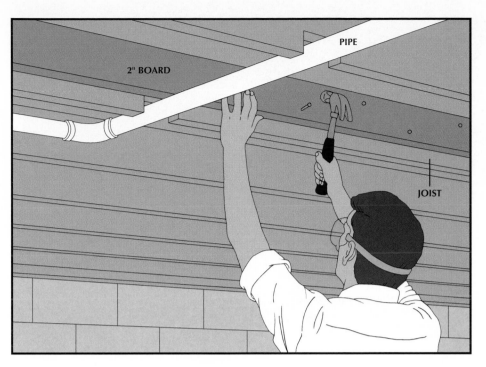

Doubling a notched joist.

◆ To reinforce a joist notched to make way for a pipe, measure the distance between the top of the obstacle and the subflooring.

◆ From the widest 2-inch lumber that will fit in the space, cut two pieces the same length as the weak joist.

◆ With a helper to hold the boards against the subflooring, fasten one of them to each side of the weak joist with $2\frac{1}{2}$-inch nails. If no helper is available, support the boards on nails driven partway into the old joist.

REPLACING A JOIST

1. Mounting a new joist.

◆ Plane or chisel the ends of the new joist to make notches (inset, opposite).

◆ Remove bridging, insert spacing blocks, and then jack up the floor (page 15).

◆ Take out any nails and blocks holding the old, weak joist to the girder and the sill plate. Remove the spacing blocks that are next to the weak joist.

◆ Apply construction adhesive to the new joist's top, then position it so the weak joist is sandwiched between the new one and the sound existing joist that extends to the opposite sill plate.

◆ Force the new joist tightly against the subfloor by driving hardwood shims at the notches (above).

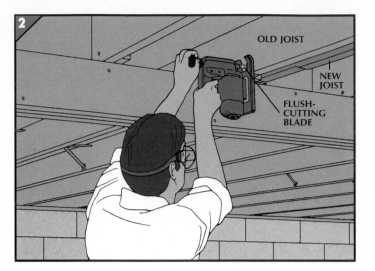

2. Removing the old joist.

◆ Cut through the weak joist at points near the girder and the sill plate with a reciprocating saw or a saber saw fitted with a flush-cutting blade.
◆ With a pry bar, lever the joist away from the nails that hold it to the subfloor.
◆ Trim protruding nail points with a plierslike cutter called a carpenter's nippers.

3. Splitting out the joist ends.

◆ With a wood chisel, split the ends of the joist that remain on the girder and sill plate *(right)*. Remove the pieces and protruding nails with a pry bar. Drive the claw of a cat's paw beneath any embedded nailheads with a hammer, and then pull on the bar to withdraw the nail.
◆ If there are breaks in the subfloor, install and shim a second new joist in the old one's place *(see Step 1)*.

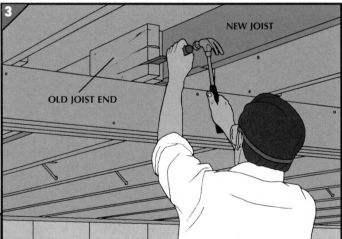

4. Nailing the joists.

◆ With $3\frac{1}{2}$-inch common nails, nail the new joists to the one they sandwich at the girder.
◆ Then nail 2-by-4 spacers every 3 feet between the new joists *(left)*.
◆ Toenail the new joists to the girder and sill plate.
◆ Trim the spacing blocks *(page 16)* to fit in the space that lies between each new joist and its neighbor, then toenail the spacers in place.
◆ Drive 3-inch finishing nails, spaced 8 inches apart, through the finish floor and into each joist.

A Stand-In for a Failing Post

When a girder sags at the top of a wood post, the trouble is in the post, not the girder. Either the post's concrete footing has sunk or the post itself has been attacked by rot or termites. Both problems have the same solution: Replace the post with a steel column that is supported by a new footing.

You will need a building permit, and some of the work involved is strenuous: removing the old wood post, breaking through the basement slab with a rented electric jackhammer, digging a hole, and pouring a new footing.

If your house is built on fill or if the span between posts is more than 12 feet, consult an architect or a civil engineer before undertaking this project.

A Steel Replacement: Adjustable steel columns, available at lumberyards and building-materials dealers, are made of 11-gauge, 3-inch

pipe fitted with a threaded base like that of a telescoping jack. Get a column 4 inches longer than the distance between the basement slab and the bottom of the girder, so the base will be anchored in concrete when you patch the slab.

The Key to a Sturdy Post: A post is only as strong as its footing. The size and depth of the footing depend on the load it must bear, on soil conditions and, in unheated basements or crawlspaces, on the depth of the frostline—the point of deepest penetration of frost below ground level.

A footing that is 2 feet square and 22 inches deep is typical, but check your local building code for the required dimensions and whether steel reinforcement is mandatory. Either rent a concrete mixer or, if you are pouring more than one footing, have concrete delivered in a ready-mix truck.

 TOOLS

House jacks
Hacksaw
Electric jack-
hammer

Masonry trowel
Shovel
Electric drill with
$\frac{3}{8}$" bit
Carpenter's level

 **MATERIALS**

Plywood ($\frac{1}{2}$")
Common nails
($2\frac{1}{2}$")
Adjustable steel
column

Lag screws (3" x $\frac{3}{8}$")
and washers
Epoxy bonding
agent
Concrete

SAFETY TIPS

When operating a jackhammer, wear goggles, gloves, ear protection, and a dust mask.

1. Removing the old post.

◆ To make way for the new column, set up telescoping house jacks *(page 15)* 3 feet to either side of the post. Raise the girder $\frac{1}{16}$ inch a day until the post no longer supports any weight.
◆ Remove the nails or lag screws that fasten the post to the girder. With a helper, tilt the top of the post clear of the girder and lift the post off the vertical steel dowel that connects it to the concrete *(right)*.

If the girder is spliced over the post, reinforce the splice before jacking the girder. Using a hacksaw, cut away any metal splice reinforcement, and nail a 3-foot length of $\frac{1}{2}$-inch plywood across the splice, on both sides of the girder. Secure each plywood piece with 30 $2\frac{1}{2}$-inch common nails.

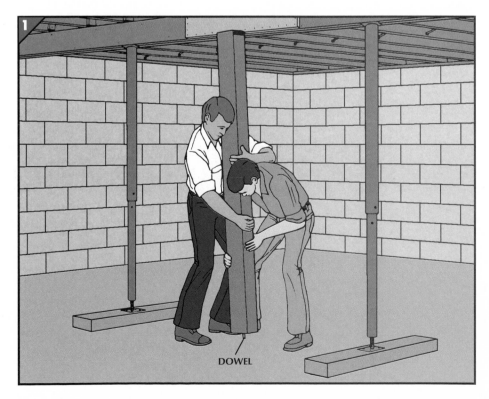

DOWEL

2. Digging the footing.

◆ On the basement floor, mark off a footing of the size that is required by your building code. Rent an electric jackhammer to break through the concrete slab.

◆ Beginning inside one of the footing marks and working toward the line, break out easy-to-handle chunks of concrete with a series of cuts. Hold the jackhammer perpendicular to the slab at the start of each cut; then, when you have chiseled out a groove, tilt the handles slightly toward yourself and lean firmly.

◆ When you have broken up the slab and the old concrete footing within the marks, dig a hole of the depth required by the code.

3. Pouring the footing.

◆ Clean out all loose dirt from the hole and spray it with a hose.

◆ While the hole is still wet, fill it with concrete to a point 4 inches below floor level. Drive a shovel into the wet concrete several times to eliminate air bubbles, then level the surface with a masonry trowel.

◆ The concrete must cure for about 2 weeks: Cover it with polyethylene sheeting, and keep the surface wet by sprinkling it with water twice a day.

4. Bolting the column.

◆ Set the steel column on the new footing. Holding the bottom plate with your toe, turn the column on its threaded base to raise the top plate tightly against the girder.

◆ Center the plate at the marks left by the old post. Using the holes in the plate as a guide, drill $\frac{3}{8}$-inch pilot holes into the girder *(above)*.
◆ Attach the plate loosely to the girder with 3-inch lag screws and washers.

5. Making the column fast.

◆ Tap the base of the column with a hammer as needed to make the column plumb, checking all sides with a level *(left)*, then tighten the lag screws.
◆ Lower the temporary jacks $\frac{1}{16}$ inch a day until they can be removed.
◆ To finish the floor around the column, coat the footing and the edges of the slab with an epoxy bonding agent. Then fill the hole with concrete to the level of the surrounding floor, and trowel it smooth.

A wood girder that sags in one place can be jacked straight and supported with a new steel post *(pages 19-21)*. Several sags, however, are a sign of a weak girder. Since girders must support all the floors above them and part of the roof, multiple sags are serious indeed. The most practical remedy is to replace the weakened girder with one made from laminated veneer lumber, or LVL *(box, below)*.

Maneuvering Girder Boards: Continuous boards make the strongest girder but may be impossible to get into the basement without your making a hole in the foundation. For a basement less than 20 feet wide, however, cutting the boards as shown on page 24 may permit you to carry them through doorways and down stairs.

Building the New Girder: Measure the width of the basement and add 4 to 6 inches for the ends to rest in the foundation wall. Take your measurements to a lumber-yard, and they will calculate how many LVL boards you need to build your beam, usually three.

Before beginning work, obtain a building permit. Thereafter, the first step is to support the floor, sag and all, with a framework of 4-by-4 shoring on both sides of the weakened girder *(opposite)*. After cutting out the old girder, bring the new boards inside and assemble the replacement girder. Finally, rebuild the foundation wall under the girder to support it.

 TOOLS

Hammer
Combination square
Saw
Tape measure
Cold chisel
Circular saw
House jacks

Mason's trowel
Joint filler
Mason's hammer
Brick set
Mason's hawk

 **MATERIALS**

2 x 6s
2 x 4s
4 x 4s
LVL boards
Double-headed
  nails (2½")
Common nails (3½")

Wood screws (2½")
Pine shims
Steel or slate shims
Rafter ties
Flashing
Concrete block
  (8 x 8)
Mortar
Bricks

 **SAFETY TIPS**

Wear goggles when hammering, sawing, using a chisel, mixing mortar, or cutting brick. Leather-palmed work gloves protect your hands from rough edges of brick or stone. Irritants in mortar call for a dust mask when mixing it, as well as gloves when applying it. Wear a dust mask when chiseling concrete block. Protect your head with a hard hat when working near joists or with heavy objects overhead.

LAMINATED VENEER LUMBER

Nowadays, many builders make girders, beams, and headers from laminated veneer lumber (LVL) instead of ordinary lumber or steel I-beams. As shown in the photograph at right, LVL is a form of plywood manufactured by gluing sheets of thin veneer together under heat and pressure. Colored wax applied to edges keeps out moisture.

LVL boards have the same thickness as 2-inch lumber and can be ordered up to 16 inches wide and 80 feet long. Lighter than steel and stronger than regular lumber, this material can be cut, nailed, drilled, and shaped with common woodworking tools and is light enough that two people can handle most boards.

PUTTING UP SHORING

1. Building the shoring.

◆ Lay straight 4-by-4s end to end across the floor to form a top plate as long as the girder. Place several shorter 4-by-4s nearby to serve as bottom plates.

◆ Mark post positions every 4 feet along the top plate (Xs), beginning 2 feet from the wall. Mark corresponding positions on the bottom plates.

◆ Find the lowest point of the sag (page 15). Measure from the bottom of the joists to the floor at that point, then cut 4-by-4 posts 7 inches shorter than this distance, to fit between the top and bottom plates.

◆ Toenail the posts to the top plate at the marks you have made, using four $2\frac{1}{2}$-inch double-headed nails per post. Or drive $2\frac{1}{2}$-inch dry-wall screws with an electric drill.

◆ Build a second framework in the same way.

BOTTOM PLATE

TOP PLATE

POSTS

2. Nailing the shoring in place.

◆ Set the bottom plates on the floor, parallel to the girder and 3 feet to either side of it.

◆ Have two helpers set the first section of top plate and posts on the bottom plate at the marks made in Step 1.

◆ Make sure the posts are plumb—if necessary, tap them into position with a hammer—then nail or screw the posts to the bottom plate.

3. Shimming the framework tight.

◆ Insert wedge-shaped pine shims under each joist (inset) from both sides of the top plate. Then hammer the wedges so they are tight (right).

◆ Erect additional sections of shoring to create a wall-to-wall framework on each side of the girder.

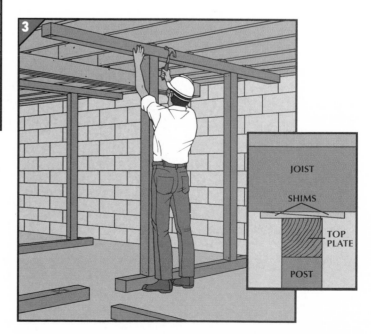

JOIST

SHIMS

TOP PLATE

POST

4. Fastening the joints.

◆ Toenail or screw top-plate sections together *(left)*, and add a post under each joint, fastening it to both sections of the top plate.

◆ Tighten shims that have worked loose.

◆ Pull out the nails that fasten the joists to the old girder, then saw the girder into pieces, cutting it 1 foot from both foundation walls and each post. To prevent pieces of girder from falling on you, have helpers support each piece as you complete the saw cuts.

◆ Pull the end pieces out of the girder pockets, then remove the posts and the 2-foot sections of girder still attached to them *(page 19)*.

INSTALLING THE NEW GIRDER

1. Chiseling out the block.

◆ Outline girder pockets enlarged to accept the LVL boards if you can bring them into the basement through existing openings. Otherwise, substitute for one pocket an access hole two courses (16 inches) tall and 8 inches wide.

◆ For both girder pockets and access holes, chip at the block with hammer and cold chisel to a depth of 4 to 6 inches *(right)*. Punch a hole through the wall at the center of the access hole. Redraw the outline on the outside, using the hole as a reference point.

◆ Complete chiseling from outside. Work behind the siding if necessary, and excavate if the second course of block is below ground level.

◆ If the blocks are hollow, fill the cores at the bottoms of girder pockets and the access hole with mortar.

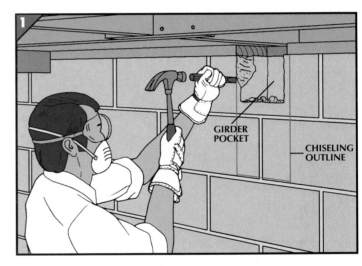

A GIRDER FROM STAGGERED BOARDS

You may be able to cut girder boards into segments that are small enough to maneuver into position without chipping a hole through your foundation wall. For this technique to work, at least two supporting posts are required. If you have more than two posts, select the the two that result in the shortest boards. In basements with only one post or none, you might find the idea of adding posts more appealing than breaking through the foundation wall *(page 20)*.

The key to a strong girder is to cut the LVL boards so that the joints fall atop posts, staggered as illustrated below. Note that one post supports a single joint; the other post supports two. Also, each board is cut into two pieces, not more.

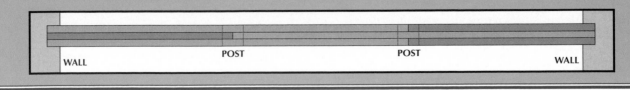

24

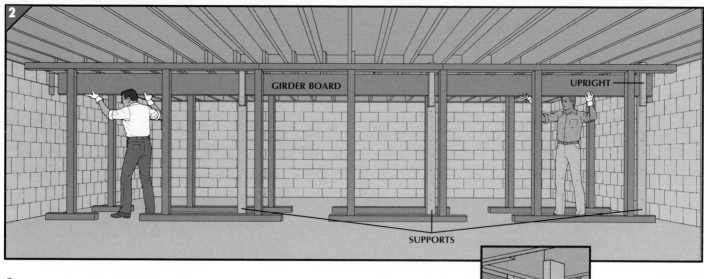

GIRDER BOARD

UPRIGHT

SUPPORTS

2. Sliding the boards into place.

◆ First construct three temporary supports to hold the boards while you slide them into position and nail them together. Each support consists of two 2-by-6s cut 1 inch shorter than the distance between the floor and the bottom of the girder, then nailed together to form a T *(inset)*. Two 2$\frac{1}{2}$-foot

lengths of 2-by-4 nailed to one end of the T hold the LVL boards on edge.
◆ Stand one support near the hole in the wall, and the others near, but not at, the post locations *(above)*.
◆ Slide the first board through the wall from outside, and place it on the supports and the far sill. Tack the board to the supports to hold it in place.

SECOND
BOARD

FIRST BOARD

SUPPORT

3. Nailing the boards together.

◆ Slide the second board onto the supports and the far sill, even with the ends of the first board.
◆ Nail the two boards to each other from each side with four 3$\frac{1}{2}$-inch nails per foot *(left)*.
◆ Position the third board alongside the first two, and nail it to the second board using the same pattern.

4. Nailing on the flashing.

Wrap aluminum flashing around each end of the girder where it will come in contact with wet mortar.

◆ First bend the flashing so it covers the bottom of the girder and both sides. Use two pieces if necessary.

◆ Next slide on the flashing, either from the basement or from outside the house. Also, cover the exposed end of the girder if you made a hole in the wall.

◆ Tack or nail the flashing on both sides and the end to secure it *(left)*.

FLASHING

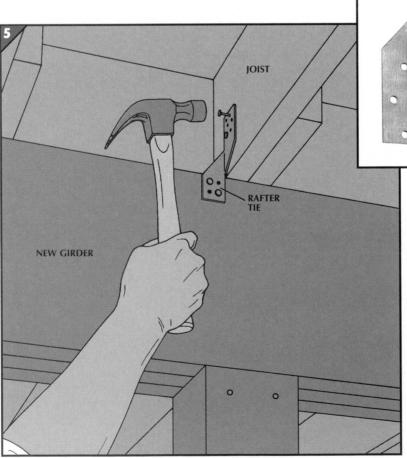

JOIST

RAFTER TIE

NEW GIRDER

5. Nailing hangers to the joists.

◆ Jack up the girder with telescoping house jacks until it touches most of the joists. Shim beneath the joists that are not touching the girder, as shown on page 23.

◆ Reinstall the posts you removed in Step 4 on page 24.

◆ At every other joist, nail a rafter tie *(photograph)* to the girder and joist that crosses it *(left)*, hammering a nail into each hole in the tie.

SUPPORTING GIRDER ENDS

1. Blocking the hole from outside.

◆ Spread mortar on top of the exposed block.

◆ Butter one side of the 8-by-8 block with mortar, and place it onto the exposed block.

◆ Wedge the two outside corners of the block upward with brick chips to keep the block even with the others.

◆ Fill the other side joint with mortar using a joint filler. Smooth the joints with a trowel.

◆ Lay the second 8-by-8 block on top of the first in the same way.

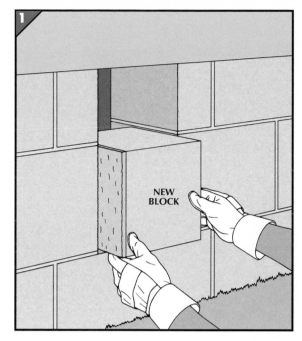

NEW BLOCK

TRICKS OF THE TRADE

Wedging with Dowels

To make mortar joints around a new block match the thickness of the joints in the rest of the wall, buy a length of dowel that is equal in diameter to the height of the mortar joints. Cut two short pieces and arrange them as shown at right, set back from the face of the wall. Place the block on top of the dowels, then fill the gaps around the block with mortar using a joint filler and mason's hawk *(below)*.

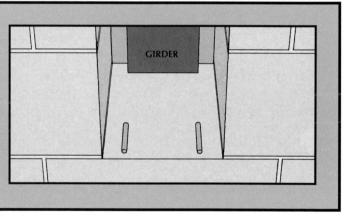

GIRDER

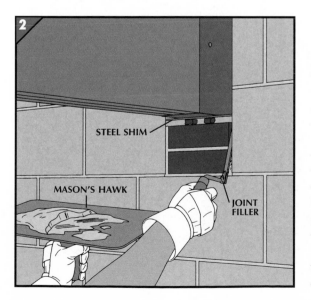

STEEL SHIM

MASON'S HAWK

JOINT FILLER

2. Bricking up the inside.

◆ With a mason's hammer and a brick set, trim bricks about 1 inch shorter than the width of the space below the girder.

◆ Lay mortar on the sill, and center the first brick in the hole. Tap it down with the trowel handle.

◆ Push mortar from a mason's hawk with a joint filler into the spaces on either side of the brick.

◆ Butter the top of the first brick, place a second brick on the mortar, then fill the side gaps with mortar *(left)*.

◆ When the gap under the girder is less than 1 inch, wedge a steel or slate shim up against the girder with brick chips. Then pack mortar under the shim.

A New Face for a Wood Floor

Restoring the natural beauty of a wood floor, whether it is varnished or painted, necessitates removal of the old finish before the new one can be applied. The first step is to take all furniture out of the room and to seal drapes in plastic bags. Lift off floor registers and cover the vents with plastic.

Fasten loose boards and replace badly damaged ones *(pages 11-13)*. Drive protruding nailheads $\frac{1}{8}$ inch below the floor surface with a nail set. Beginning at a door, remove shoe moldings from baseboards by driving the nails through the molding with a pin punch no larger than the nailhead.

Getting to Bare Wood: Some laminated floorboards are too thin to sand; remove the old finish with a chemical stripper. On thicker boards, use a drum sander *(below)*. Multiple sandings are required.

For rough or painted floorboards, begin with 20-grit sandpaper, then proceed to 36-grit, 50-grit, and finally 80-grit. Varnished or shellacked floors need only three sandings beginning with 36-grit. Sand parquet floors first with 50-grit followed by 80- and 100-grit.

Removing Stains: First try to remove a stain by hand-sanding. If it remains, apply a small amount of wood bleach to its center. Let the spot lighten, then apply enough bleach to blend the treated area with the rest of the floor. Rinse away the bleach with a vinegar-soaked rag. If the stains remain even after bleaching, replace the boards *(pages 11-13)*.

A Two-Step Glaze: To protect the wood and emphasize the grain, apply a sealer, which is available in both natural wood hues and a clear, colorless form *(page 30, bottom)*. For a final protective glaze over the sealer, select a urethane floor finish, which becomes exceptionally tough as it hardens.

Both oil- and water-based sealers and finishes are available. If you plan to stain the floor, oil-based products provide richer, more even color than water-based products, which dry faster and are easier and safer to handle.

If you choose water-based products, apply and smooth them with tools made of synthetic material, avoiding natural-bristle brushes and steel wool. Use a synthetic abrasive pad instead. Clean the floor with a lint-free rag rather than a tack cloth.

⚠️ **CAUTION** *Sanding produces highly flammable dust. Seal the doorways into the work area with plastic, and ventilate the room with a fan (opposite).*

TOOLS

Nail set
Pin punch
Drum sander
Edging machine

Floor polisher
Paint scraper
Paintbrushes
Lambs wool
  applicator
Putty knife

MATERIALS

Sandpaper
Wood bleach
Vinegar
Tack cloth
Lint-free rags

Sealer
Urethane floor
  finish
Abrasive pads
  (steel-wool or
  synthetic)
Tinted wood putty

SAFETY TIPS

Sand floors wearing goggles, ear protection, and dust mask. When applying wood bleach, sealer, or finish, put on goggles and rubber gloves, as well as long pants and a long-sleeve shirt.

TOOLS TO RENT

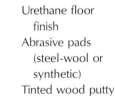

A refinishing job calls for professional equipment. One such tool is a drum sander *(right)*. Make sure the machine has a tilt-up lever for lifting the spinning drum from the floor (not all have this feature). The second is an edging machine, a sander with a rotating disk for working along baseboards and other places that the drum sander cannot reach. Finally, to smooth each coat of sealer or new finish, rent a commercial floor polisher. Fit it with a round pad of steel wool—or a synthetic abrasive pad if using a water-based finish.

Before leaving the shop, check that the machines are working and that their dust bags are clean. Take with you any special wrenches for loading the drum sander and plenty of sandpaper—at least 10 drum-sander sheets and 10 edger disks of each grit for an average room. Because sanders need grounding, they must have three-pronged plugs; if your house has two-slot receptacles, you will need grounding adapters.

1. Loading the drum sander.

◆ With the sander unplugged, thread a sheet of sandpaper into the loading slot, turn the drum one full revolution, and slip the other end of the sheet into the slot.

◆ To secure the paper, tighten the drum's internal clamp by turning the boltheads at both ends of the drum with the wrenches provided by the dealer. With fine-grit sandpaper, fold a strip of the material in half, grit exposed, and slip it into the slot between the two ends to keep them from slipping out *(inset)*.

TRICKS OF THE TRADE

Filtered Ventilation

A window fan with a furnace filter helps clear the air in a room while you are sanding. Buy a filter large enough to cover the entire fan, and tape it to the intake side; duct tape works well for the purpose. Place the fan in a window with the intake side inward, and turn it on. The filter will catch a large portion of the dust so it does not collect in your fan or blow into the neighborhood.

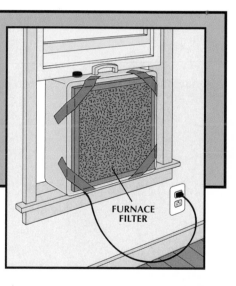

2. The first sanding.

◆ Standing with a wall about 3 feet behind you, lift the drum from the floor with the tilt-up lever, start the sander, and when the motor reaches full speed, lower the drum to the floor. Let the sander pull you forward at a slow, steady pace. Sand boards along the wood's grain unless they undulate slightly. In that case, or if the floor is patterned with varying grain directions, do the first sanding diagonally.

◆ At the far wall, raise the drum from the floor, move the cord behind you to one side, then lower the drum and pull the sander backward over the area you just sanded.

◆ Lift the drum and move the machine to the left or right, overlapping the first pass by 2 or 3 inches.

◆ Continue forward and backward passes across the room, turning off the sander occasionally in order to empty the dust bag, then turn the machine around and sand the area next to the wall.

⚠ **CAUTION** *Keep the sander in motion to prevent it from denting or rippling the wood.*

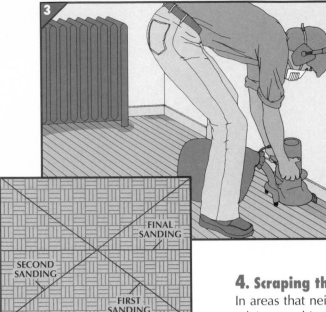

3. Completing the sanding.

◆ Sand areas missed by the drum sander with the edger, loaded with coarse-grit paper.

◆ Repeat both the drum and edge sandings, with successively finer sandpaper. On floorboards, these sandings, like the first, should be made with the grain. On parquet floors, do the second sanding on the opposite diagonal to the first, and the final sanding along the length of the room *(inset)*.

◆ Smooth the floor with a floor polisher *(opposite)* and a fine abrasive pad, suited to sealer and finish. This will lessen the boundary between drum- and edge-sanded areas.

4. Scraping the tight spots.

In areas that neither the drum sander nor the edging machine can reach, remove the finish with a paint scraper. At a radiator, remove collars from around the pipes for a thorough job. Always pull the scraper toward you, applying firm downward pressure on the tool with both hands. Scrape with the grain wherever possible, and replace the blade when it gets dull. Sand the scraped areas by hand.

APPLYING PROTECTIVE COATS

1. Spreading sealer.

◆ Ventilate the room. Vacuum the floor and pick up dust with a tack cloth, or a dry rag if using water-based sealer.

◆ Starting next to a wall and away from the door, apply sealer liberally over a 3-foot-wide strip of floor with a rag. Use long, sweeping strokes along the grain of the wood or along the length of the room if the grain directions vary.

◆ Between 8 and 20 minutes after it is applied, the sealer will have penetrated the wood, leaving shallow puddles of the liquid on the surface. Have a helper, using rags in both hands, mop up the excess sealer.

◆ As your helper works on the first strip, start applying sealer to the second strip. Try to work at a pace that keeps both of you moving together with your knees on dry floor until the job is almost finished. On the last strip, the helper will have to back across wet sealer to the door.

◆ Finally, let the sealer dry according to the manufacturer's specifications.

2. Smoothing the sealed wood.

ABRASIVE PAD

SCRUB BRUSH

◆ Fit a floor polisher with a heavy-duty scrub brush and press a fine abrasive pad into the bristles of the brush *(inset)*. Run the polisher over the floor to smooth irregularities in the surface caused by tiny bubbles in the sealer coating.

◆ Scour the edges and corners of the floor by hand with a small abrasive pad, then vacuum the entire floor and go over it thoroughly with a tack cloth or damp rag, according to the finish, to pick up any remaining dust.

3. Finishing the floor.

◆ Apply the finish slowly and evenly with a wide brush. With oil-based finish you may use a lambs wool applicator *(photograph)*. Work along the grain. If grain directions vary, work along the room's length. Stroke in one direction and do not go back over finish that has begun to set. If working alone, do edges and corners first with a small brush, then work on the rest.

◆ When the first coat is dry, smooth the surface *(Step 2, above)*.

◆ Clean the floor with a vacuum and tack cloth or damp rag. Force wood putty, tinted to match, into cracks and nail holes with a putty knife.

◆ Apply a second coat of finish in the same way. Water-based urethane, thinner than oil-based, needs a third coat.

◆ Wait 24 hours. Replace shoe moldings, registers, radiator-pipe collars.

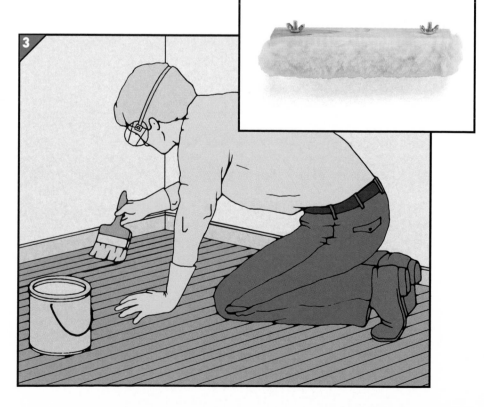

The tough surface of resilient flooring—typically vinyl tiles or sheet flooring—will resist wear and stains for many years. If damage does occur, you can usually repair it yourself, or at least reduce the visibility of the scars.

Common-Sense Precautions: A resilient floor should be kept as dry as possible, even when being cleaned, so that water does not get underneath and destroy the bond of the adhesive that holds it in place.

Resting furniture feet on plastic or rubber coasters will help protect the floor from punctures and gouges. When heavy furniture or appliances must be moved across the floor, slide them over pieces of plywood.

Curing Minor Ailments: To conceal a shallow scratch in a vinyl floor, gently rub it lengthwise with the rim of an old coin. This will press the edges of the scratch together so only a thin line remains. Deeper cuts can be closed by carefully heating the vinyl with an iron and aluminum foil, as explained on page 35.

If a tile has come loose, first determine whether water from leaking plumbing is the cause; if it is, repair the leak before fixing the floor. Use water-based latex adhesive to glue the tile down.

Mending Major Flaws: The best remedy for a ruined tile is a replacement; similarly, a badly damaged section of sheet flooring will need a patch. But before removing any resilient flooring or adhesive, read the asbestos warning on page 34.

If you cannot find any spare matching tiles or sheet flooring, look for replacements in inconspicuous areas of your floor—under a refrigerator or at the back of a closet, for instance. Cut and remove the section from the hidden area and substitute a nonmatching material of equal thickness.

If your resilient floor is glued to an asphalt-felt underlayment, the felt may tear as you remove damaged flooring. Usually you can glue the felt back together with latex adhesive; allow the adhesive to dry before continuing the job. If the felt is too badly torn, cut out the damaged section and glue down enough replacement layers of 15-pound asphalt felt to maintain the same floor level.

 TOOLS

Putty knife
Utility knife
Iron

Notched trowel
Metal straightedge

 **MATERIALS**

Latex adhesive
Replacement vinyl tiles or sheet flooring

 **SAFETY TIPS**

Protect your hands with rubber gloves when working with adhesive.

SIMPLE FIXES

Securing a loose tile.
◆ Lift the loose portion of the tile and spread a thin coat of latex adhesive on the underside of it with a putty knife. If only a corner of the tile has come unstuck, loosen more of it until you can turn the tile back far enough to spread the adhesive.
◆ Press the tile into place, so that it is level with those tiles that surround it. Hold it down with a 20-pound weight for at least an hour.

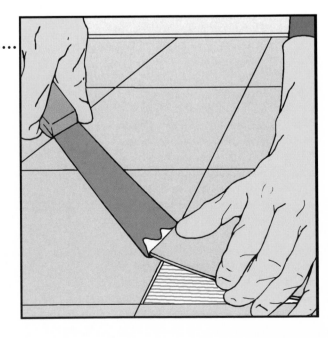

Deflating a blister.

◆ Following a line in the flooring pattern if possible, score then slice along the length of a blister with a utility knife *(right)*. Extend the cut $\frac{1}{2}$ inch beyond the blister at both ends.

◆ With a putty knife, spread a thin layer of latex adhesive through the slit onto the underside of the flooring.

◆ Press the vinyl down; if one edge overlaps because the flooring has stretched, use it as a guide to trim the edge beneath. Remove trimmed-off scrap, then press the edges together and put a 20-pound weight on the repaired area for at least 1 hour.

Dealing with Stains

Most resilient flooring today has a permanent finish as hard, smooth, and shiny as wax, protecting it against stains and dirt. Daily sweeping plus occasional damp-mopping is usually sufficient to remove grime. Limit washing with detergent and water to every 3 to 6 weeks.

Over time, some spillage and staining is almost inevitable. The following treatments are recommended for stains caused by common substances:

STAIN	REMEDY
Alcoholic beverages	Go over the spot with a cloth that has been dampened with rubbing alcohol.
Blood	Sponge with cold water; if that does not work, sponge with a solution of 1 part ammonia to 9 parts water.
Candle wax, chewing gum, or tar	Cover with a plastic bag filled with ice cubes. When the material becomes brittle, scrape it off with a plastic spatula.
Candy	Rub with liquid detergent and grade 00 steel wool unless the floor is a "waxless" vinyl; in that case use a plastic scouring pad, warm water, and powdered detergent.
Cigarette burns	Rub with scouring powder and grade 00 steel wool.
Coffee and canned or frozen juice	Cover for several hours with a cloth saturated with a solution of 1 part glycerine (available at drugstores) to 3 parts water. If the stain remains, rub it gently with scouring powder on a damp cloth.
Fresh fruit	Wearing rubber gloves, rub with a cloth dampened with a solution of 1 tablespoon oxalic acid, a powerful solvent available at hardware stores, and 1 pint water.
Grease and oil	Remove as much as possible with paper towels, then wash the stain with a cloth dampened in liquid detergent and warm water.
Mustard or urine	Cover for several hours with a cloth soaked in 3 to 5 percent hydrogen peroxide, and cover that cloth with another soaked in household ammonia.
Paint or varnish	Rub with grade 00 steel wool dipped in warm water and liquid detergent.
Leather and rubber scuff marks	Scrub with a cloth soaked in a solution of 1 part ammonia to 9 parts water.
Shoe polish or nail polish	Rub with grade 00 steel wool soaked in warm water and scouring powder.

REPLACING A DAMAGED TILE

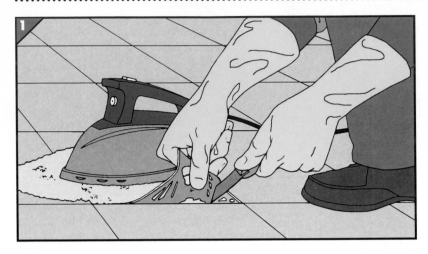

1. Removing a tile.
◆ Lay a towel on the tile and warm it with an iron at medium heat until the adhesive softens and you can lift one corner with a putty knife.
◆ Pull up the corner and slice at the adhesive underneath with the putty knife, reheating the tile with the iron if necessary, until you can take out the entire tile.
◆ Scrape the remaining adhesive from the sub-floor (see asbestos warning below).

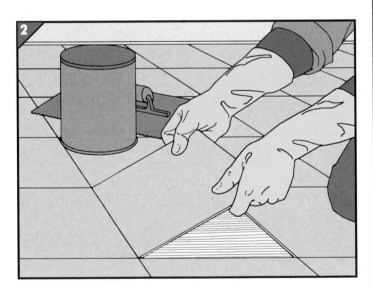

2. Installing a replacement.
◆ Spread a thin layer of adhesive—not more than half the thickness of your tile—on the subfloor with a notched trowel, then butt one edge of the new tile against the edge of an adjoining tile, aligning the pattern.
◆ Ease the tile into place. Make sure it is level with surrounding tiles; if it is too high, press it down and quickly wipe away excess adhesive before it dries; if the tile is too low, gently pry it out with a putty knife and add more adhesive beneath it. Rest a 20-pound weight on it for the length of time specified by the adhesive manufacturer.

> ## ⚠ CAUTION
>
> ### Asbestos Warning
>
> *If your resilient floor was installed before 1986, the flooring or the adhesive underneath may contain asbestos. When damaged, these materials can release microscopic asbestos fibers into the air, creating severe, long-term health risks. Unless you know for certain that your floor does not contain asbestos, assume that it does, and follow these precautions when making any repairs:*
>
> **!** *Always wear a dual-cartridge respirator. Asbestos fibers will pass right through an ordinary dust mask.*
>
> **!** *Never sand resilient flooring or the underlying adhesive.*
>
> **!** *Try to remove the damaged flooring in one piece. If it looks likely to break or crumble, wet it before removal to reduce the chance of raising dust.*
>
> **!** *When scraping off old adhesive, always use a heat gun to keep it tacky or a spray bottle to keep it wet.*
>
> **!** *If vacuuming is necessary, rent or buy a wet/dry shop vac with a HEPA (High Efficiency Particulate Air) filtration system.*
>
> **!** *Place the damaged flooring, adhesive, and HEPA filter in a polyethylene trash bag at least 6 mils thick, and seal it immediately.*
>
> **!** *Contact your local environmental protection office for guidance as to proper disposal.*

PATCHING SHEET FLOORING

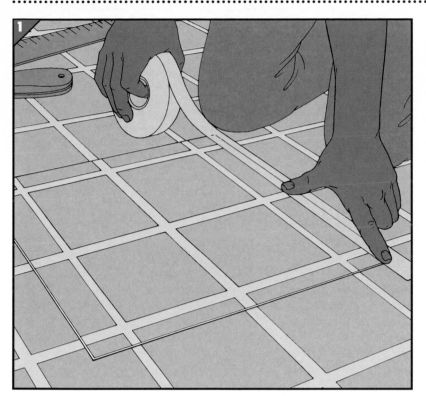

1. Cutting the patch.

◆ Place over the damaged spot a spare piece of matching flooring larger than the area to be patched, aligning the design of the replacement piece with that of the floor. Secure it in position with tape *(left)*.

◆ With a metal straightedge and a utility knife, score the top piece, following lines in the pattern where possible. Using the scored line as a guide, cut through the replacement piece and the flooring underneath. Keep slicing along the same lines until you have cut through both sheets.

◆ Set the replacement piece aside and loosen the adhesive under the section you are replacing as shown in Step 1 on page 34. Remove the damaged section and the old adhesive.

2. Installing the patch.

◆ Spread adhesive over the exposed subfloor with a notched trowel and set the replacement patch in position as you would a tile *(page 34, Step 2)*.

◆ Hide the outline of the patch by a careful application of heat: Cover the edges of the patch with heavy aluminum foil, dull side down, and press the foil several times with a very hot iron *(inset)*. This will partly melt the cut edges of the flooring so they form a solid and almost undetectable bond.

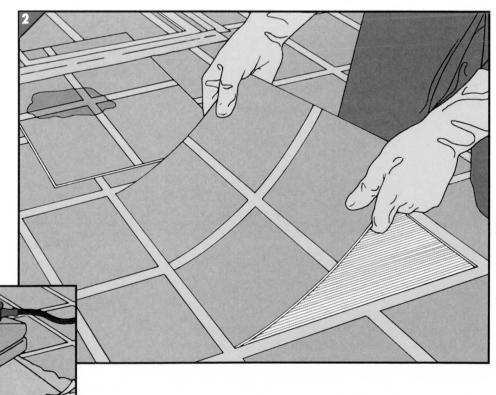

Concrete and marble, slate or ceramic tiles make the most durable floors. They are also the most inflexible and brittle. All of them can be cracked by the fall of a heavy weight. They can also be pulled apart by the normal expansion and contraction of a house.

Underlying Problems: A floor that is cracked throughout a room is usually a sign of trouble in the structure beneath it. If your subflooring is less than $1\frac{1}{8}$ inch thick, you may have to replace it.

When subflooring has localized damage, you can usually tighten or patch problem areas. Repair the cause of any water damage before installing new flooring. Dampness in concrete slabs may not be curable; dry the area as much as possible, and use a waterproof epoxy adhesive to hold the finish surface in place.

Ceramic Tiles: The techniques for replacing a tile at the base of a toilet *(below and opposite)* work for repairing damage around any permanent fixture, such as a tub, pipe, or kitchen cabinet.

Use organic adhesives to lay new tile on a wood subfloor or on smooth, dry concrete, and epoxy adhesive on a floor that is moist or uneven. Fill joints between tiles with color-matched silicone grout, which comes premixed in squeeze tubes, cures quickly, and adheres to both old and new tile.

Marble and Slate: These tiles are normally butted tightly against each other in a bed of mortar. To cut them, use a saber saw with a tungsten carbide blade instead of scoring the tile as a prelude to fracturing it or shaping it with tile nippers *(opposite, bottom)*. Otherwise, replacing them involves only slight variations in the procedure for ceramic tiles shown here.

Concrete: Fill cracks less than an inch wide with a vinyl or latex patching compound. Use concrete and wire mesh for larger cracks *(pages 38-39)*, and apply an epoxy bonding agent to the old concrete before pouring the patch. This prevents the old, dry concrete from absorbing water the new concrete needs for proper curing.

TOOLS

Grout saw	Grease pencil
Straightedge	Tile nippers
Glass cutter	Carbide-tipped
Electric drill	hole saw
Masonry drill bit	Adhesive spreader
Hammer	Sledgehammer
Cold chisel	Shovel
Compass	Wire brush
	Metal shears
	Trowel

MATERIALS

	Bricks
Replacement tile	Reinforcing wire
Emery cloth	Patching concrete
Tile adhesive	Epoxy bonding
Grout	agent
Length of 2 x 4	Plywood sheet
Gravel ($\frac{3}{4}$")	Bucket
	Polyethylene

SAFETY TIPS

Safety goggles will protect your eyes when you remove tiles, grout, or concrete. Wear rubber gloves when spreading adhesives, and work gloves when breaking up old concrete and mixing or finishing new concrete.

A TIGHT FIT AROUND A FIXTURE

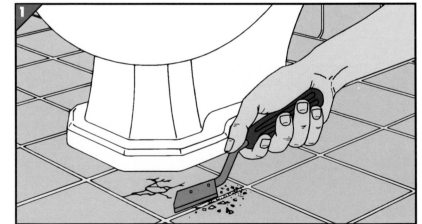

1. Removing the grout.
◆ Run a grout saw along the joints bordering the damaged tile, applying firm pressure as you move the saw back and forth.
◆ To remove grout from very narrow joints, unscrew one of the twin blades supplied with the saw. For extra-wide joints, add a third blade.
◆ Clean fine debris and dust from grooves with a brush or shop vacuum.

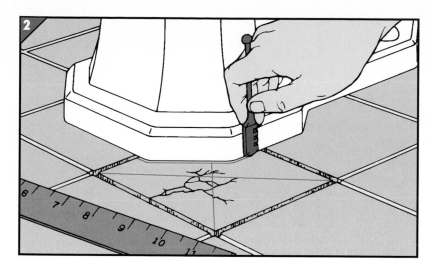

2. Taking out the tile.

◆ For ceramic tile, score an X on the damaged piece with a glass cutter and straightedge, then score along the base of the fixture *(left)*.
◆ Drill a hole through the center of the X with a $\frac{1}{4}$-inch masonry bit. Hammer a cold chisel into the hole, and working toward the edges, break the tile into small pieces. Remove the tile fragments, and scrape off the old adhesive beneath them with a putty knife.

On marble or slate tile, mark an X with a grease pencil. With a masonry bit, drill $\frac{3}{4}$-inch holes every $\frac{1}{2}$ inch along the X and the fixture's base. Break out the tile with a hammer and chisel.

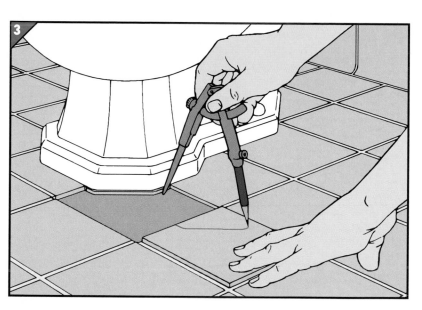

3. Marking the new tile.

◆ Lay a new tile over the tile adjacent to the space you have cleared.
◆ Replace the pencil in a school compass or scribe with a grease pencil, and open the compass to the width of a tile.
◆ Set the pencil at the edge of the new tile and the point of the compass or scribe at the corresponding point on the base of the fixture.
◆ Holding the new tile securely, move the compass slowly along the base of the fixture to mark the shape of the base on the new tile.

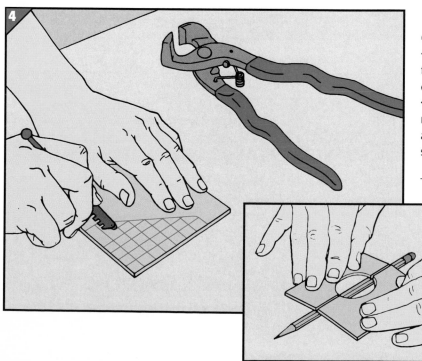

4. Cutting the tile.

◆ Score the fixture outline with a glass cutter, then score a crisscross pattern in the area to be cut away *(left)*.
◆ Using only the corners of the nipper blades, nibble $\frac{1}{8}$-inch pieces of tile away from the scored area with tile nippers. Check the tile for fit, and smooth the edges with an emery cloth.

To replace tile around a pipe, mark the pipe diameter on adjacent edges of the tile, draw lines across the tile, and drill a hole at the center of the square thus formed with a carbide-tipped hole saw. Using a glass cutter, score the tile through the center of the hole, then set the tile on a pencil and break the tile by pressing on both sides *(inset)*.

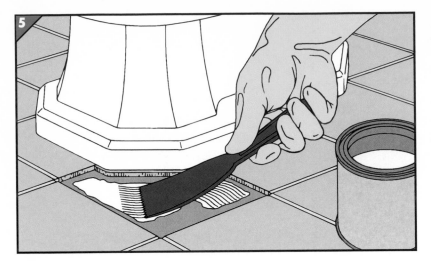

5. Setting the tile in place.

◆ With a notched plastic spreader, apply adhesive to the subfloor or mortar bed. If the new tile has tabs on its back, also add a thin coat of adhesive to the bottom.

◆ Apply enough adhesive to raise the tile slightly higher than the ones around it. Use toothpicks or coins set on edge as spacers to keep the joints between ceramic tiles open and even.

◆ Lay a 2-by-4 across the tile, and tap it down with a mallet or hammer.

◆ Let the adhesive set for 24 hours, remove the spacers, and fill the joints with silicone grout.

DURABLE PATCHES FOR CONCRETE

1. Preparing the area.

◆ Break up the damaged concrete with a sledgehammer or an electric jackhammer (page 20). Cut reinforcing wire in the broken concrete with metal shears and clear away the debris.

◆ With a cold chisel and a hammer, slope the edge of the hole toward the center. Then dislodge loose particles of concrete with a wire brush and remove them.

◆ Dig out the top 4 inches of dirt from the hole and tamp the bottom with the end of a 2-by-4. Fill the hole to the bottom of the slab with clean $\frac{3}{4}$-inch gravel.

2. Reinforcing the patch.

◆ Unroll wire reinforcing mesh over the hole, and cut it with metal shears so that the ends of the wires rest on the sloped edge of the hole.

◆ Reinforcing mesh usually comes in rolls 5 feet wide; if you are patching a wider hole, wire two pieces of mesh together.

◆ Place the mesh in the hole supported by bricks.

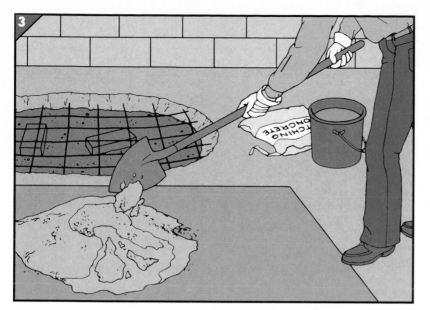

3. Pouring the patch.

◆ Form a cone of premixed patching concrete on a piece of plywood or in a mortar pan. Hollow out the top and add water as specified by the manufacturer. Mix the ingredients thoroughly *(left)*.

◆ Coat the edges of the hole with an epoxy bonding agent. Before the coating dries, shovel the concrete into the hole. Jab with the shovel tip to force the mix against the sides of the hole and through the reinforcing mesh.

◆ Fill the hole to the level of the slab, then add a few extra shovelfuls to allow for settling.

4. Finishing the patch.

◆ With a helper, work a straight 2-by-4 across the surface of the patch with a back-and-forth motion. Fill any surface depressions with concrete and smooth the patch again.

◆ A thin film of water will soon appear on the surface. When it evaporates and the surface sheen disappears, smooth the patch with a metal trowel. To trowel a large patch, kneel on boards laid across it and work backward, moving the boards as you go.

◆ When the concrete hardens, sprinkle it with water and cover it with polyethylene. Let the patch cure for 3 to 7 days, checking it daily and sprinkling it as needed to keep the surface damp.

MAINTAINING THE LOOK OF YOUR CONCRETE FLOOR

After patching the concrete, you can leave your floor unfinished or apply a protective coating to its surface. Penetrating sealers are the least expensive finishes for concrete. They can be easily applied, dry in about 8 hours, and leave a thin film that protects against stains.

You will need to remove stains that might spoil the rough beauty of raw concrete or prevent a finish coat from adhering. Many stains can be scrubbed away with a household detergent. Those listed here require special treatment. To remove these stains, first fold a piece of cheese-cloth several times and lay it over the affected area. Then pour the recommended cleaning agent over the cloth. The chemicals will dissolve the stain, and the cheesecloth will absorb the chemicals.

RUST: 1 part sodium citrate to 6 parts glycerin.

GREASE, OIL, OR MILDEW: 1 pound trisodium phosphate to 1 gallon of water.

COPPER, BRONZE, OR INK: 1 part ammonia to 9 parts water.

IRON: 1 part oxalic acid to 9 parts water.

OLD PAINT: use a commercial paint remover.

New Floors: A Wealth of Choices

When installing a floor, select the material best suited to the demands of the room. Resilient flooring—so called because it cushions the impact of feet or objects—is ideal for high-traffic areas. Wood is more expensive but provides a feeling of warmth. Stone or ceramic tiles offer unsurpassed durability and are less vulnerable to water damage in potentially damp areas, such as entryways or bathrooms.

A pneumatic power nailer →

Readying a Room for a Wood Floor

The amount of work involved in laying a new wood floor depends on the material of your old floor. The boards of an existing wood floor must be removed. Ceramic tile floors also must be removed—and a new subfloor installed *(below)*—before laying the new boards. Old resilient sheet or tile flooring demands less work; simply re-cement loose flooring *(page 32)*. The preliminaries are even more involved, however, if the subfloor is in poor condition or if you are laying the boards over a concrete slab.

Handling a Damaged Subfloor: Pulling up an old wood floor will expose any ruined subflooring, but resilient flooring can hide damage that would undermine a new wood floor. If the old floor feels soft, peel back the flooring to check the plywood underneath, observing the asbestos precautions on page 34. Cut out the damage and patch the hole with plywood of the same thickness. In severe cases, remove the entire subfloor, repair any structural damage *(page 14)*, then lay a new subfloor *(below)*.

A New Subfloor: Check the joists before installing a subfloor. If they are more than 16 inches apart or are smaller than 2-by-8s, reinforce them *(pages 16-17)*, or install additional joists between the old ones. In attics built for light storage, it may be necessary to use $\frac{3}{4}$-inch plywood for the subfloor instead of the customary $\frac{5}{8}$-inch material.

Concrete Floors: Before trying to floor a concrete slab, check it for excess dampness by laying a 16-inch-square piece of plastic trash bag on the slab and sealing the edges with tape. If condensation occurs after several days, the concrete is a poor choice for a wood floor. Even a dry slab, however, needs a moisture barrier *(opposite)* under a new subfloor, unless you plan to glue the boards to the concrete *(page 49)*.

 TOOLS

Caulk gun	Maul (2 pound)
Chalk line	

 **MATERIALS**

Construction adhesive	Wood-to-concrete adhesive
C-D grade plywood ($\frac{5}{8}$")	Pressure-treated boards (1 x 2)
Dry-wall screws	Masonry nails ($1\frac{1}{2}$")
2 x 4s	Polyethylene film (4 mil)
Lag screws ($\frac{3}{8}$") and washers	Ring underlay nails (2")
Masonry primer	

SAFETY TIPS

Pressure-treated wood contains arsenic compounds as preservatives. Wash your hands thoroughly after handling this wood, and wear a dust mask when sawing it.

Laying a new subfloor.

◆ Make a dry run, staggering joints and leaving $\frac{1}{8}$ inch between sheets and along walls. Where sheets meet at a joist, make sure there is a bearing surface for both.

◆ Apply enough construction adhesive to the joists or sleepers for a single sheet *(right)*, then lay the sheet down.

◆ Secure each sheet with dry-wall screws driven into the joists every 10 inches, except at the edges that run along joists. There, drive the screws $\frac{3}{8}$ inch from the edges, 6 inches apart, and stagger them with those in the adjacent sheet.

◆ To support the subfloor's outer edges, add cleats as necessary to joists hidden beneath walls; nail one or more 2-by-4s to each concealed joist *(inset)* to provide a $\frac{1}{2}$-inch bearing surface. Secure the boards to the joist at 16-inch intervals with lag screws fitted with washers.

Floating a Floor to Reduce Noise

To help muffle the sounds of footsteps on a floor overhead, you can adapt the "floating floor" techniques used to soundproof apartment buildings.

Glue $\frac{1}{2}$-inch insulation board, available from lumberyards in 4- by 8-foot sheets, to the existing floor or subfloor with clear silicone caulk. Attach 1-by-3 furring strips to the board with construction adhesive, placing the strips between joists. Then fasten a $\frac{1}{2}$-inch plywood subfloor to the furring strips *(right)* and install the finish flooring. If you are planning to replace the subfloor and wish to subdue noise further, lay insulating batts between the exposed joists.

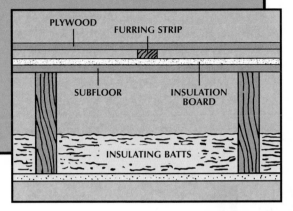

A MOISTURE BARRIER

1. Laying bottom sleepers.

◆ Sweep the floor clean and apply a coat of masonry primer.

◆ When the primer dries, snap chalked lines 16 inches apart across the short dimension of the room.

◆ Cover each line with a 2-inch-wide ribbon of adhesive intended for bonding wood to concrete.

◆ Embed random lengths of pressure-treated 1-by-2s, or sleepers, in the adhesive, leaving a $\frac{1}{2}$-inch space between the ends of the boards.

◆ Use a 2-pound maul to secure the sleepers with $1\frac{1}{2}$-inch masonry nails about 24 inches apart.

2. Attaching the top sleepers.

◆ Lay sheets of 4-mil polyethylene film over the sleepers, overlapping joints 6 inches.

◆ Fasten a second course of 1-by-2s to each first course with ring underlay nails, sandwiching the film between the two layers.

Installing a New Wood Floor

Wood flooring is durable and elegant in appearance yet remarkably simple to install because of interlocking tongues and grooves milled on the sides and ends of the boards. Some are lumber, others are laminated. Laminated boards may be glued down instead of nailed, and either type may be purchased prefinished or sanded and finished after installation.

Nailing Techniques: All nailable floors must be installed over a wood subfloor *(page 42)*. In cases where boards are face-nailed, nails are countersunk and concealed with wood putty. Most often, however, the boards are blind-nailed through their tongues to hide the nailheads *(page 12)*.

To speed the work, rent a power nailer, either an automatic or a manual model like the one shown on page 46. You may need an accessory called a wedge adapter for the nailer to fasten $\frac{1}{4}$- to $\frac{3}{8}$-inch-thick laminated boards. On prefinished flooring, wrap the bottom of the tool with duct tape to protect the finish. Before using the nailer on your floor, practice on a scrap of flooring atop some spare plywood.

An Alternative to Nails: Glue-down boards can be affixed directly to almost any smooth, dry surface, including concrete, provided it is free of coatings such as paint and wax that might interfere with the adhesive. Fill in low spots in your concrete slab with flash patch, a cement-sand-epoxy compound. If the slab fails the dampness test *(page 42)*, hire a professional to lay a moisture barrier.

Until you've gained the experience of laying several courses of flooring, spread no more than 40 square feet of glue, or mastic, at a time. And when cutting pieces to fit, work in another room to avoid mixing sawdust with the mastic.

Before You Begin: Prepare the existing surface of the floor as described on pages 42 to 43.

Because wood floorboards, especially those made of lumber, are susceptible to warping and swelling caused by moisture, take delivery of the flooring at least 3 days in advance. Make sure your home is at its normal humidity level, then untie the bundles and stack the boards in loose piles to let them adjust to the climate in the room.

 TOOLS

Circular saw	Carpenter's nippers
Dovetail saw	Power nailer and
Chalk line	mallet
Tape measure	Pry bar
Electric drill with	Hand-screw clamps
$\frac{1}{16}$" bit	Miter box
Hammer	Backsaw

 **MATERIALS**

Asphalt-impregnated	Shoe molding ($\frac{3}{4}$")
building felt	Slip tongue
(15-pound)	Wood-flooring
Tongue-and-groove	mastic
flooring	1 x 2s
Finishing nails	Masonry nails
($2\frac{1}{2}$", $1\frac{1}{2}$")	V-notch trowel
Clamshell reducer	Carpenter's glue
strips	Flooring roller
Corkboard ($\frac{3}{4}$")	(100-pound)

 **SAFETY TIPS**

When working with mastic, keep the room well ventilated, and wear rubber gloves while spreading the adhesive. Protect your eyes from flying debris when hammering and sawing, and use earplugs to reduce the noise of the circular saw.

HOW TO BUY HARDWOOD FLOORING

Wood flooring is rated in order of decreasing quality and price as "clear," "select," "No. 1 common," or "No. 2 common," depending on color, grain, and imperfections such as knots and streaks. The boards are sold according to a "flooring board foot" formula, based on their premilled size. To determine the amount of flooring you need, calculate the area of your room in square feet. For $\frac{3}{4}$- by $2\frac{1}{4}$-inch boards, the most common size, multiply the area by 1.383 to convert to flooring board feet and to account for waste. For boards of other dimensions, ask your flooring distributor for the proper conversion factor.

1. Trimming for a new floor.

◆ Shorten each door that opens into the room to account for the new floor height. To do so, simulate the new floor with boards laid next to the doorstop. Add the height of a threshold if you plan to install one—plus $\frac{1}{4}$ inch for clearance above the finished floor—and mark the door. If the door is veneered, score the cut with a utility knife to prevent splintering while sawing.

◆ Using the straight factory edge of plywood as a guide, cut along the marked line.

◆ Cut the doorstop and doorcasings even with the flooring using a flush-cutting dovetail saw *(page 61, photo)*. If adding a threshold, position it on top of the flooring and trim the doorstop to that height.

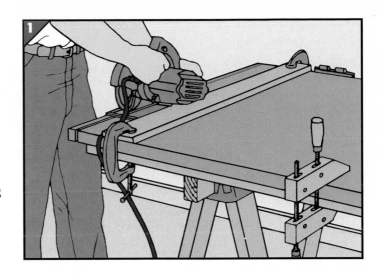

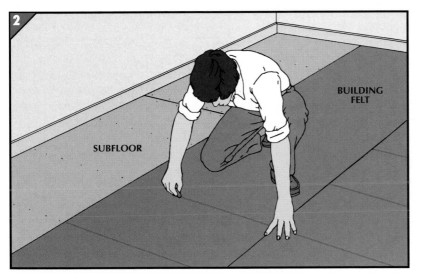

SUBFLOOR

BUILDING FELT

2. Marking the joists.

◆ Choose a wall that runs perpendicular to the joists as the starting wall along which you will lay the first course.

◆ Along the wall opposite the starting wall, unroll a strip of asphalt-impregnated building felt.

◆ On the felt, mark the positions of the joists, using the nailing pattern as a guide if there is a plywood subfloor. If the joists are hidden by existing flooring, and if they cannot be seen from below, use a stud finder to locate them.

◆ Continue unrolling strips of felt—overlapping them 3 inches and marking the joists—until the floor is covered.

3. Aligning the starter course.

◆ Find the midpoints of the walls parallel to the joists and snap a chalk line between them to mark the center of the room.

◆ Measure equal distances from the ends of the centerline to within roughly $\frac{1}{2}$ inch of the starting wall and snap a starting chalk line between those points *(right)*. Laying the starter course along this line ensures that boards in the center of the room look straight even if the room is not quite square. Shoe molding will hide the gap between the first course and the baseboard *(page 48, Step 7)*.

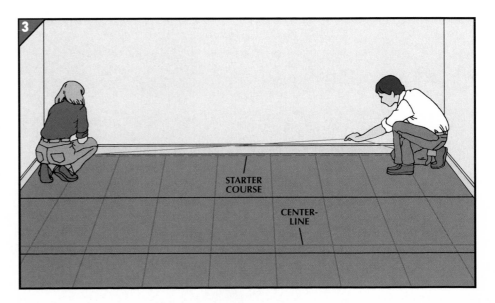

STARTER COURSE

CENTER-LINE

NAILING THE BOARDS

1. Face-nailing the starter course.
◆ An inch from each end of a long flooring board and an equal distance from the grooved side, drill a $\frac{1}{16}$-inch pilot hole.
◆ With a helper, align the grooved side of the board along the starting chalked line, $\frac{1}{2}$ inch from the side wall to allow a gap for expansion.
◆ Countersink a $2\frac{1}{2}$-inch finishing nail through each pilot hole.
◆ Drive and countersink more nails through pilot holes drilled at every joist and midway between them, about an inch from the grooved edge.
◆ Nail the rest of the first course, interlocking tongue and groove ends, and finishing with a piece that fits within $\frac{1}{2}$ inch of the side wall.

2. Arranging the field.
◆ Working out from the starter strip, rack seven or eight loose rows of flooring boards, staggering end joints in adjoining rows at least 6 inches apart and leaving a $\frac{1}{2}$-inch gap along the walls.
◆ Secure the second and third courses, fitting grooves onto tongues, tapping them in place with a mallet and protective block if necessary. Blind-nail them along joist lines.

3. Using the power nailer.
◆ At the fourth course, slip the power nailer's head onto the tongue of the first board, about 2 inches from the wall. Strike its plunger with a rubber mallet to drive a nail through the board's tongue and into the subfloor (inset).
◆ Using your heel to keep the board fitted tightly against the preceding course, drive nails into the tongue at each joist, halfway between joists, and near the board's end. Use carpenter's nippers to snip off nails that do not penetrate completely.
◆ Install boards with the nailer until you get too close to the wall to use it, then blind-nail the remainder by hand.

FLOORING NAIL

4. Installing the final boards.
◆ If more than $\frac{1}{2}$ inch of space remains at the far wall, trim boards on the tongue side to fill the gap *(page 48)*.

◆ Drill pilot holes *(page 46, Step 1)*, then position the board on the floor.

◆ Insert a pry bar between the flooring board and the baseboard *(right)*, protecting the baseboard with a scrap of wood. Push the pry bar sideways with your foot to hold the board in place and face-nail the board to joists and the subflooring.

REDUCER STRIP

5. Finishing off a doorway.
Drill pilot holes, then face-nail a clamshell reducer strip—so called because its rounded top makes it resemble half a clamshell—at a doorway where a new wood floor meets a lower floor. The reducer strip *(photograph)*, available at flooring distributors, is milled on one side to fit over the tongue of an adjoining board. The strip can also be butted to the ends of floorboards that run at right angles to a doorway.

6. Laying expansion strips.
Wedge strips of $\frac{3}{4}$-inch corkboard into the space where the floor meets glass sliding doors, ceramic tiles, or a laid stone floor. The cork acts as a cushion that compresses or expands to compensate for shrinkage or swelling of the floorboards.

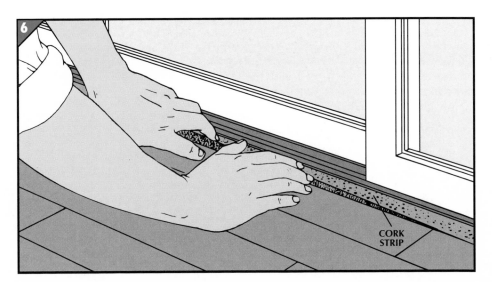

CORK STRIP

7. Installing shoe molding.

◆ Through the center of $\frac{3}{4}$-inch shoe molding, drill $\frac{1}{16}$-inch pilot holes that are angled to direct a nail into the baseboard.

◆ Fasten the shoe molding over the gap between the flooring and the baseboard with $1\frac{1}{2}$-inch finishing nails.

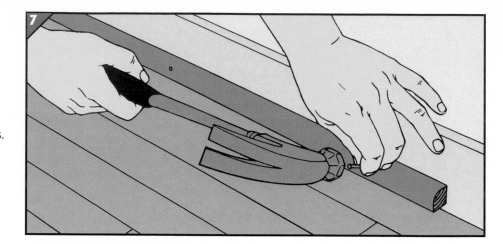

SPECIAL SITUATIONS

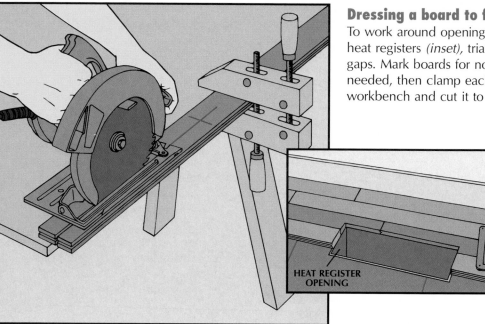

Dressing a board to fit.

To work around openings in the floor, such as heat registers (inset), trial-fit boards over the gaps. Mark boards for notching or trimming as needed, then clamp each board securely to a workbench and cut it to fit.

HEAT REGISTER OPENING

Framing special borders.

Using a miter box, saw boards at 45-degree angles to frame a fireplace hearth (inset). Remove the boards' tongues when necessary to make them fit tightly against adjoining boards, then face-nail them into place.

Reversing tongue direction.

To blind-nail tongue-and-groove boards in a hall or closet opening onto the groove side of the starting course, join groove to groove with a slip tongue, available in 3-foot lengths from flooring distributors. Place the slip tongue into the back-to-back grooves, then position the power nailer over the tongue of the loose board and nail it to the floor.

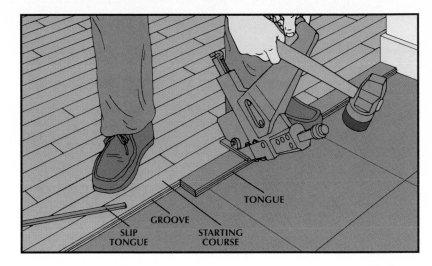

SECURING BOARDS WITH GLUE

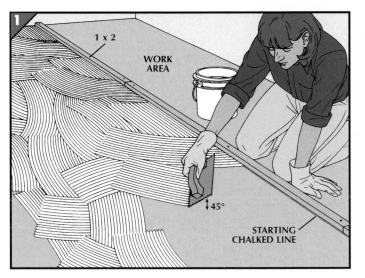

1. Spreading the mastic.

◆ Establish a starting chalked line *(page 45, Step 3)* approximately 30 inches from the starting wall. The 30-inch gap serves as a mastic-free work area.

◆ Snap a parallel chalked line as a boundary for spreading mastic for the first courses of boards, remembering not to exceed 40 square feet.

◆ Fasten 1-by-2s along the starting chalked line with masonry nails. They will hold the first course in place while you add succeeding rows, so be sure they are straight.

◆ With a V-notch trowel held at a 45-degree angle, spread mastic between the chalked lines.

◆ Wait for the mastic to become tacky, usually 20 minutes to an hour.

2. Affixing the boards.

◆ At the left end of the starting chalked line, lay a board $\frac{1}{2}$ inch from the wall, tongue side against the 1-by-2s. Tap it with a mallet and protective block to seat it in the mastic.

◆ Apply carpenter's glue sparingly to the tongue end of the next board, fit it in the groove of the first board, and lay the board along the 1-by-2s. Seat it in the mastic, then remove excess glue with a damp cloth.

◆ Continue the first course until you are within 4 feet of the wall, then cut the last board to fit, leaving a $\frac{1}{2}$-inch gap between it and the wall.

◆ Add boards by rows, cutting pieces as necessary to stagger joints *(page 46, Step 2)*. Interlock the sides first, then the glued ends, before seating the board in the mastic.

◆ Fill in the rest of the room, removing the 1-by-2s and flooring the work area last.

◆ Use a flooring roller to bond the boards securely to the mastic, then let it set as the adhesive label advises.

Tiling a Floor in Wood or Vinyl

Tile flooring, whether it is made of wood, linoleum, or some synthetic material such as vinyl, lends itself to imaginative design. Moreover, it can be glued to almost any surface. Before laying the tiles, however, you must plan the pattern of the floor and prepare the surface as described in the introduction to "Installing a New Wood Floor" on page 44.

Resilient Tiles: Tiles of vinyl and its relatives come in a vast array of colors, styles, and patterns. Some are available as 12-inch squares, others as 9-inch squares. However, aside from following the instructions that begin at the bottom of this page for planning your floor on graph paper and laying it, there is little about such tiles that requires particular attention.

Wood Parquet: Some aspects of wood tiles require special consideration. They are available, for example, not only as squares, but also as rectangles. This feature

permits patterns like the ones shown on page 53, which are impossible with resilient tiles.

Grain also needs to be considered. All the tiles can be laid with the grain in the same direction, but results are often more attractive if grain direction alternates from one tile to the next.

Because wood tiles absorb moisture, allow them 72 hours to adjust to the humidity before laying them. Also, to allow for expansion, leave a $\frac{1}{2}$-inch space between the border tiles and the walls, then fill it with a strip of $\frac{1}{2}$-inch cork, covered by quarter-round molding. In areas that are heavily trafficked, such as doorways, lay a border of whole tiles on the sides of the room where there are doors; partial tiles tend to loosen in the heavy foot traffic there.

> ⚠️ **CAUTION** *Use a nonflammable, latex-based tile adhesive, and keep the room well ventilated.*

 TOOLS

Chalk line
Flooring roller
  (100-pound)
V-notch trowel
Utility knife
Mallet
Fine-toothed
  handsaw

 **MATERIALS**

Graph paper
Small nails
Tape measure
Adhesive for vinyl
  or wood tiles
Wood block
Cork strip ($\frac{1}{2}$")

 **SAFETY TIPS**

When spreading adhesive, wear rubber gloves.

INSTALLING RESILIENT TILES

1. Planning on paper.

◆ On graph paper, plot a design for a floor laid on the square *(near right)* or on the diagonal *(far right),* letting each block represent one tile if they are square (or the width of the tile if they are rectangular). If you plan to use 9- rather than 12-inch tiles, multiply the dimensions of the room by 1.33 to find how many tiles to plot to a side. Always count fractions as whole tiles.

◆ Buy one 12-inch tile for each square foot to be covered. To determine how many 9-inch tiles to purchase, multiply the room's square footage by 1.78. For two colors of tile, subtract the squares of one color from the total to see how many tiles you need of each; add 5 percent for waste and repairs.

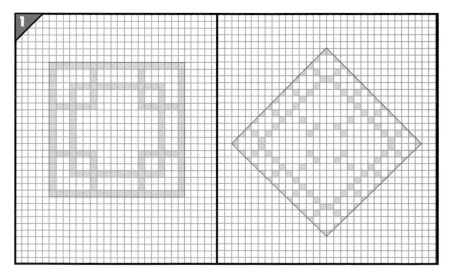

2. Guidelines for the dry run.

◆ Divide the room into equal quadrants with two chalked strings that are stretched between nails set at the midpoints of facing walls.

◆ Make sure that strings are perpendicular by measuring 3 feet from the intersection on one string and 4 feet on the other. The diagonal between the 3- and 4-foot points should be exactly 5 feet. Do not snap the chalk lines yet.

For a diagonal pattern, measure from the intersection to one of the two longer walls, and transfer the distance to the wall on both sides of the guideline nail. Then set nails into the wall. Do the same thing on the facing wall, and stretch chalked strings diagonally between the nails *(inset, red lines).*

3. Making a dry run.

For a pattern laid on the square—including the Haddon Hall pattern for wood parquet *(page 53)*—place dry tiles along the guidelines defining one quadrant, starting from the intersection and duplicating the plan on your graph paper. If both rows end more than half a tile from the walls, snap the chalk lines.

If the border is less than half a tile, shift the rows so you will not have to cut and lay small pieces. Set the chalk lines in the new place and snap them.

To check a diagonal pattern, lay tiles corner to corner along the lines defining one quadrant, and lay another row along the diagonal guideline *(inset).*

When laying a diagonal or herringbone pattern *(page 53)*, arrange for the pattern to end in a sawtooth line of half tiles; add a border of tiles set on the square to fill any space between a wall and the nearby half tiles. If differences in the widths of borders on two adjacent walls are visually disturbing, make the borders at least two tiles wide.

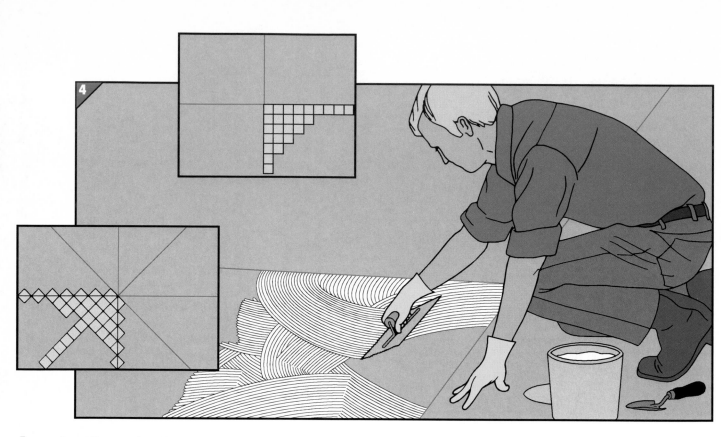

4. Setting tiles and adhesive.

◆ Apply adhesive holding the notched trowel so it is at a 45-degree angle. If you are laying tiles on the square, spread adhesive along one chalked line. Work from the intersection toward a wall, leaving parts of the line uncovered for guidance. Let the adhesive become tacky.

◆ Lay this row of tiles, butting each tile against one already laid and dropping it into place. Press the tile firmly against the adhesive.

◆ Beginning again at the intersection, set a row of tiles at a right angle to the first, then fill in the quadrant as shown in the upper inset.

◆ When you have finished a quadrant, roll it with a rented flooring roller.

To lay a diagonal pattern *(lower inset),* set tiles point to point over the perpendicular chalked lines. Lay another row of tiles with their sides along the diagonal chalked line. Then fill in the area between rows, working from the intersection toward the wall.

5. Trimming a border tile.

◆ Place two loose tiles squarely on top of the last whole tile in a row and slide the upper one across the untiled gap until it touches a wall.

◆ Using the edge of the top tile as a guide, score the one beneath with a utility knife. Snap the tile along the scored line and fit the piece into the gap, snapped edge against the wall.

◆ Trim door moldings to permit tiles to slip under them, and cut tiles to fit around cabinets or other obstacles *(page 37).*

For a diagonal pattern, score tiles from corner to corner and snap them, forming triangular half tiles to fill the sawtooth edge of the pattern. Trim tiles for a square-set border as at left.

LAYING WOOD PARQUET

Setting wood tiles in place.
The procedure for laying a wood parquet floor is identical to the one described on pages 50 to 52 for resilient tile, with a couple of exceptions. First, you must use a mallet, cushioned by a block of wood, to join the tiles—which have tongue-and-groove edges like floorboards *(page 44)*—and to set them in the adhesive. While you are tapping with the mallet, hold adjacent tiles in place by kneeling on them. Second, use a pencil to mark tiles for trimming instead of scoring them, and cut them with a fine-toothed handsaw.

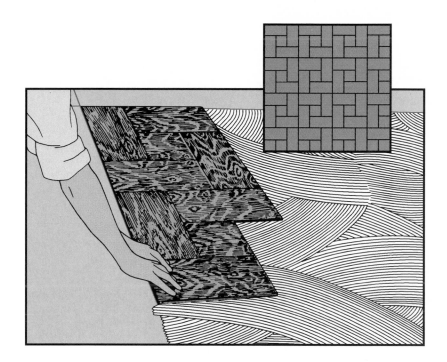

The Haddon Hall pattern.
◆ In the corner of one quadrant, lay two 6- by 12-inch tiles perpendicular to each other.
◆ Set a 6- by 6-inch tile in the corner created by the perpendicular tiles, and position two 6- by 12-inch tiles around it to make a square within a square.
◆ Complete the quadrant pyramidally, then fill in the other quadrants *(inset).*

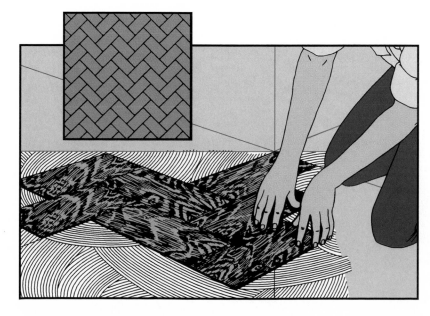

The herringbone pattern.
◆ Establish guidelines as for laying square tiles on the diagonal *(page 51, Step 2).*
◆ Spread adhesive in one quadrant, extending several inches beyond the guidelines as shown.
◆ Place a 6- by 12-inch tile along a diagonal guideline, with one corner at the intersection.
◆ Lay the second tile across the end of the first, and the third across the end of the second.
◆ Use the chalked lines and these tiles as guides for the next three tiles, and continue in this manner until you reach the wall.
◆ Repeat in the other sections of the room to complete the floor *(inset).*

A New Sheet-Vinyl Floor

Durable and stain-resistant, resilient sheet-vinyl flooring is an excellent choice for such high-traffic areas as a kitchen or playroom. It also has a great virtue as replacement flooring: In most cases, sheet vinyl can be laid right over an existing floor. Vinyl-flooring suppliers offer a variety of products to level and smooth the old surface and ensure good adhesion of the new flooring with a nonflammable, water- or latex-based adhesive. If the old floor must be removed, first read the asbestos warning on page 34.

Buying Replacement Flooring: Measure the room at its widest and longest points and add 6 inches at each wall for overlap. Because sheet vinyl comes in widths of up to 15 feet, you may be able to avoid seams. If you do need more than one sheet, buy a small bottle of seam sealer from the flooring dealer.

To fit the new vinyl flooring to your room, either purchase a pattern-making kit when you buy the flooring or use kraft paper and masking tape to make a template *(below)*.

Preliminary Steps: Move all furniture or appliances out of the room, then remove the shoe molding at the base of the walls; remove any door thresholds as well. Lay the new flooring out flat in a convenient space for 24 hours to adjust to the household temperature. The tightness of the inner part of the roll will have compressed the pattern on that part of the sheet; to even out the pattern, reverse the roll briefly.

> ⚠️ **CAUTION** *Seam sealer is toxic and flammable; follow all safety precautions on the label.*

 TOOLS

Utility knife
Straightedge
Notched spreader
Flooring roller
Screwdriver

 **MATERIALS**

Kraft paper
Masking tape
Vinyl-flooring adhesive
Seam sealer

 **SAFETY TIPS**

Protect your hands with rubber gloves when handling adhesive, and wear heavy work gloves when cutting flooring with a utility knife.

MAKING A TEMPLATE

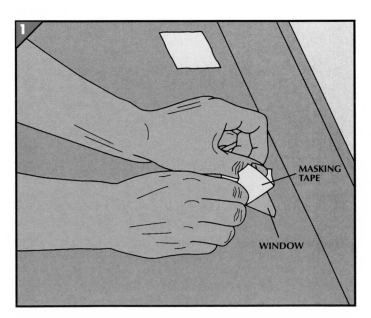

1. Taping down the template.
◆ Cut a length of kraft paper 6 inches longer than the longest floor edge. Position the paper along the floor edge $\frac{1}{8}$ inch from the wall with its ends lapped up the adjacent walls.
◆ With a utility knife, cut windows in the paper along the floor edges; then stick masking tape over the windows *(left)* to secure the paper to the flooring under it.
◆ Working across the floor to the other side, continue to lay down and tape together overlapping lengths of paper to cover the entire floor.

MASKING TAPE

WINDOW

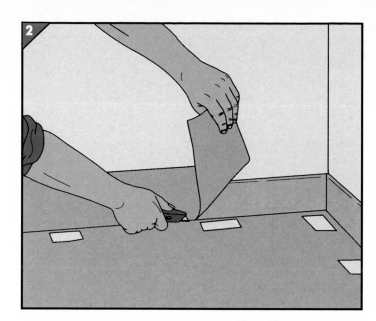

2. Trimming excess edges.

◆ With the utility knife, trim off the paper around any obstructions—radiators or built-in cabinets, for example. Then trim the paper where it is lapped up a wall *(left)*.

◆ Carefully roll up and remove the template in one piece.

CUTTING AND INSTALLING THE PIECES

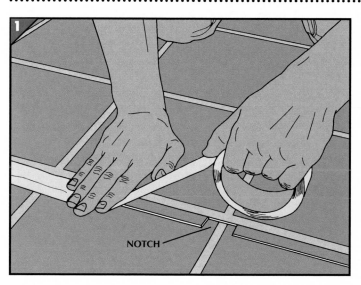

NOTCH

1. Aligning sheets for a seam.

If you need more than one sheet of replacement flooring to cover a room, you must align the patterns and secure the sheets along the seam before installation.

◆ Place the sheets flat in a work area with their seam edges butted together.

◆ With a utility knife and a straightedge, cut rectangular notches along the edge of one replacement sheet: At each pattern line perpendicular to the edge, make a notch 1 inch long and wide enough to reach to the first pattern line parallel to the edge.

◆ Pull the notched edge of the replacement sheet over the edge of the other sheet and use the notches to align their patterns.

◆ Tape the two sheets together securely with masking tape *(left)*.

2. Cutting replacement flooring.

◆ With the replacement sheet or sheets laid out flat, place the template on top of the flooring, centering it with any pattern lines.

◆ Tape the template to the flooring with masking tape. With a felt-tip pen, mark a cutting outline on the flooring around the template edges, then remove the template.

◆ Cut along the outline with a utility knife and a straightedge *(right)*; keep any excess pieces for repairs.

◆ Roll up the flooring and carry it into the room where it is to be installed. Unroll it and check the fit, trimming along the walls and doors and around obstructions, if necessary.

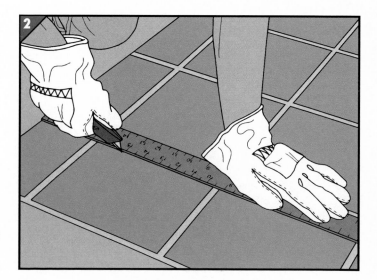

3. Adhering the flooring.

◆ Starting at one edge of the flooring along a wall, roll it back to the floor center. If there is a seam, stop 18 inches from it.
◆ With a notched spreader, coat the underlayment or the old floor evenly with adhesive

(above, left), working from the wall back to the center.
◆ Let the adhesive set for the time specified by the manufacturer. Then roll the flooring back out over the adhesive; make any small adjustments immediately.
◆ Roll a flooring roller over the

flooring *(above, right)*, making two passes at a 90-degree angle to each other. Secure the flooring edges with a hand roller.
◆ Follow the same procedure to adhere the other half of the flooring. If your flooring has no seam, proceed to Step 6.

4. Cutting a seam.

◆ Remove the masking tape from the overlapped flooring edges along the seam.
◆ On the notched sheet, lay a straightedge along the pattern line at the top of the notches.
◆ Hold the utility knife against the straightedge and make several firm, steady strokes to cut through both flooring sheets and produce clean, even edges.

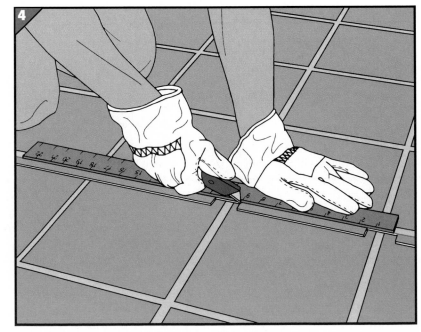

5. Adhering a seam.

◆ Pull the flooring on each side of the seam back 18 inches to expose the old flooring and coat it evenly with adhesive using a notched spreader.

◆ Allow the adhesive to set for the time specified by the manufacturer, then roll the flooring on each side of the seam back over the adhesive.

◆ Push a flooring roller back and forth over the area.

6. Finishing the installation.

◆ Keep traffic off the flooring for 24 hours after you have adhered it.

◆ Seal any flooring seam with a commercial seam sealer recommended for the flooring, following the manufacturer's instructions.

◆ Reinstall or replace the shoe molding you removed. Put back any thresholds removed from doorways, screwing them through the flooring into the underlayment *(right)*.

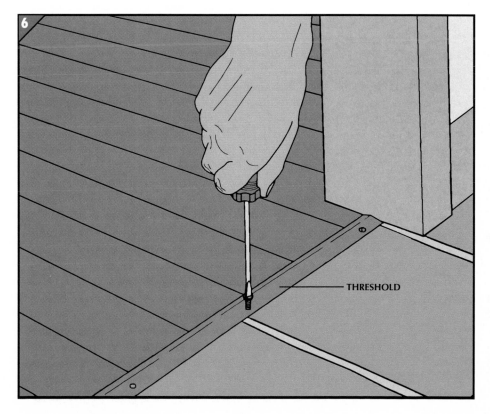

THRESHOLD

Setting Stone and Ceramic Tiles in Mortar

Rigid flooring tiles made of ceramic or a stone such as slate, sandstone, or marble offer greater durability than resilient materials like wood or vinyl. Plan a new rigid-tile floor as explained on pages 50 to 51.

When selecting floor tiles, remember that they become slippery when they are wet. Choose ceramic tiles for the floor of a bathroom, kitchen, or vestibule that have an abrasive grain fired into the glaze in order to reduce slipperiness. Marble tiles are best finished to a soft gloss rather than a high polish. Glazed ceramic tiles are impermeable, but some rigid flooring, such as Mexican and quarry tiles, absorbs liquids and therefore requires a protective sealant to make it resistant to stains.

Preparing the Surface: While rigid tiles are best laid directly on a concrete slab, as described here, you can also use them to cover an existing tile floor in good condition. Furthermore, modern adhesives make it possible to lay rigid tiles on a plywood subfloor using the methods for laying resilient tiles *(pages 50-52)*. After removing baseboards and shoe moldings, however, you'll need to build up the subfloor to a thickness of $1\frac{1}{4}$ inches. A thinner subfloor is not rigid enough to prevent the floor from flexing and cracking the tiles.

No matter what surface you tile over, it must be flat. Roll a pipe over the floor in several directions, looking for surface undulations greater than $\frac{1}{8}$ inch. Reduce high spots with a rub brick or a rented concrete grinder; fill low spots with mortar.

When tiling an area of concrete that is larger than 125 square feet, cover the concrete with an isolation membrane before laying any tiles. Available as a sheet or a thick liquid, the isolation membrane helps prevent cracks in the concrete from affecting the tiles.

Setting the Tiles: Anchored to a concrete slab with thin set—a type of mortar mix to which you add water—rigid tiles are laid with joints between them. Fill these gaps with grout containing sand if they are $\frac{1}{8}$ inch wide or larger. For smaller spaces or for marble tiles, use unsanded grout. Gray grout made with Portland cement is inconspicuous and does not show dirt, but you can also tint the grout with powdered coloring available from building-supply dealers.

Finishing the Edges: For ceramic-tile or marble-tile floors, a marble threshold is generally installed in interior doorways. Marble companies cut thresholds to length and bevel them to join the newly tiled floor to its neighbor. Thresholds for bathroom doorways should rise $\frac{1}{4}$ inch above the tiled floor to make a dam against spills. Outside doorways may need new weatherproof metal thresholds.

The job is finished, for most vestibules and hallways, with wood baseboards and base shoes—the ones you removed or new ones. For a formal look or for protection against splashes in bathrooms, make bases of the same material as the floor. Ceramic-tile makers can supply such trim.

For stone floors, you can make your own base trim by sawing 12-by-12 tiles into 4-by-12 strips. Smooth and bevel or round the rough edges with silicon-carbide sanding disks in an electric drill, using grits 80, 150, and 320 in succession. Secure the trim to the wall with thin-set adhesive.

 TOOLS

Chalk line
Square-notch
  trowel
Sponge
Mason's trowel
Level
Mallet
Circular saw with
  silicon-carbide
  masonry blade
Tile cutter
Tile sander
Dovetail saw
Grout float
Small brush
Clamps

 **MATERIALS**

Concrete isolation
  membrane
Thin-set mortar
Tile spacers
2 x 4
2 x 10
Sawhorses
Scrap wood
Grout
Grout sealant

 **SAFETY TIPS**

Be prepared for dust when cutting stone or ceramic tiles. Work outdoors if possible, and wear goggles, a respirator, and earplugs. Wear rubber gloves when spreading mortar and grout.

1. Making the mortar bed.
◆ When laying tile on bare concrete, dampen it before proceeding.
◆ Divide the room into equal quadrants and snap chalk lines as described on page 51.
◆ At the intersection of the chalked lines, use a square-notch trowel to spread a low mound of mortar, then hold the trowel nearly vertical and drag the teeth on the sub-floor, leaving ridges of mortar *(left)*. Add more of the dry ingredients if the mortar is soupy and does not form ridges. If the mortar is dry and crumbly, add water.

2. Laying the first tile.
◆ Sponge water onto the back of a tile if it absorbs water readily. Place the tile on the mortar at the intersection of the guidelines. Press it down firmly, twisting it slightly several times. Apply your full body weight on big tiles.
◆ Lift the tile off the floor and examine the bottom. If you see a pattern of ridges or that the bottom is less than 90 percent covered with mortar, use a larger notch trowel to make a new bed and re-lay the tile.
◆ With the handle of a mason's trowel, tap the tile to align it with the chalked lines.
◆ Level the tile diagonally and along two adjacent sides. Tap down any high sides with a mallet and a 2-by-4 wrapped in cloth. Scoop up excess mortar.

3. Filling in the field.
◆ Lay four tiles around the first tile to form a cross. For tiles without spacing lugs cast on their bottom edges, insert rubber or plastic tile spacers between them. Let the tiles set overnight.
◆ Fill in each quadrant, redampening bare concrete before doing so if it has dried. Since tiles may differ in size, measure frequently from the guidelines *(left)*. Enlarge spacing as needed to keep tiles aligned and rows even.
◆ As you set tiles, check their height against the center tile using a level on a straight 2-by-4. Tap down any high tiles *(Step 2)*.
◆ Use the techniques shown on page 37 to fit tiles around obstacles.

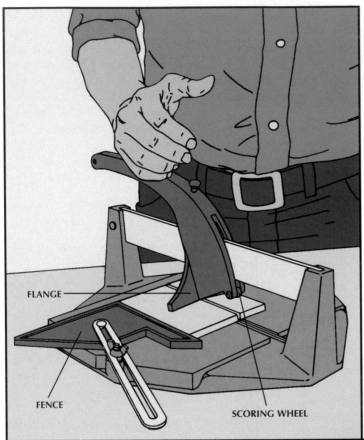

FLANGE

FENCE

SCORING WHEEL

Cutting border tiles.

Mark border tiles for cutting as described on page 52. For most ceramic tiles, rent a tile cutter *(left)*. Set the fence to position the cut line under the scoring wheel, then score the tile surface. Release the handle and gently strike it with your hand. The flanges on the tool will snap the tile along the scored line.

For stone tiles or thick ceramic ones, use a circular saw fitted with a silicon-carbide masonry blade *(below)*. Clamp the tile between a guide board and a 2-by-10 on sawhorses. Beside the tile, place wood scraps no thinner than the tile to carry the saw at the beginning and end of the cut. Cut the tile in two passes, the first $\frac{1}{4}$ inch deep, the second through the tile and $\frac{1}{8}$ inch into the 2-by-10.

> ⚠️ **CAUTION** *Cut tiles are sharp. Dull the edges with a tile sander, available from tile suppliers.*

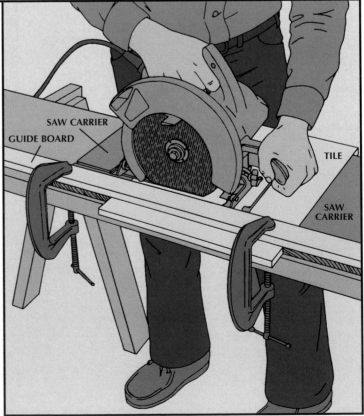

SAW CARRIER

GUIDE BOARD

TILE

SAW CARRIER

Setting a threshold.

◆ Position the threshold in the doorway and mark its height on the doorstops.

◆ With a handsaw—preferably the dovetail variety *(photograph)*—cut the doorstops at the marks.

◆ Set the threshold in a bed of raked mortar just as you would a tile.

FINISHING THE JOB

1. Spreading grout.

◆ Let the tiles set overnight, then remove the spacers between them.

◆ Pour a cup or two of premixed grout onto the tiles. Working on sections of 5 square feet or so at a time, hold a grout float at a 45-degree angle to the floor and sweep it diagonally across the joints several times, forcing grout between the tiles.

2. Packing grout into the joints.

◆ Turn the float on edge and compact the grout in each section until it is slightly below the surface of the tiles.

◆ When the floor is done, clean the float, then drag it across the surface to remove excess grout.

◆ Wipe the tiles, 10 to 15 minutes later, with a damp cloth to remove any grout haze.

◆ Keep the grout moist as it cures—usually about 3 days—then brush grout sealant over the joints and allow it to dry.

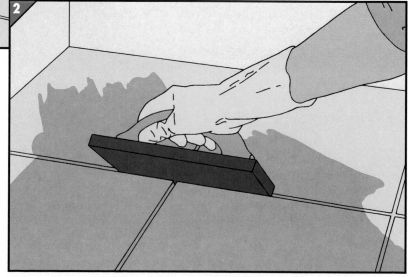

The Craftsmanship of Stairways

Stairways of all shapes and sizes share one trait: whether plain or elaborate, they must be sturdy. The most common problems—squeaky treads, loose or broken balusters—are minor and easily corrected using the techniques shown on pages 64 to 75. The rest of the chapter explains how to install a variety of new stairways, from simple steps for a basement to an elegant main staircase and balustrade.

Nailing a glue block under a stairway →

Intricate Structures, Simple to Repair

Building a stairway and balustrade goes beyond simple carpentry to include elegant techniques of cabinetwork and ingenious joinery. For this reason major problems are rare and usually caused by settling of the floor at one or both ends of the stairway, throwing it out of plumb and level and skewing its right-angle joints.

Jacking up the floor *(page 14)* may restore the stairway's health, but if the damage is extensive, have a contractor raze the old one; you can install a new prefabricated stairway yourself *(pages 90-99)*.

An Assortment of Common Ailments: The following pages offer simple solutions to squeaks, broken parts, wobbly newel posts, or worn treads. For many of these repairs you need to know how your stairway was built. Among finished interior stairways made of wood there are only two basic types *(below and opposite, top)*, defined by the way the treads are supported—rough stairways, such as a cleat stairway for the basement *(pages 86-89)*, are sometimes made by simpler methods. Metal spiral stairs *(pages 80-85)* are a special case.

Open-sided stairways with more than three steps require a post-and-railing fence, or balustrade *(opposite, bottom)*, to provide a handhold. A balustrade's many components are susceptible to minor damage and loosening over time but can also be mended easily.

Protecting the Look of Your Wood: Two precautions are in order when repairing finished-wood stairways. Treads, risers, balusters, newel posts, railings, and moldings are made of hardwood—usually oak, birch, poplar, or beech—and will split unless pilot holes are bored for all nails and screws.

Also, glue, used to repair treads and balusters, will not bond to dried glue; old joints must be scraped before reassembly. Glue can also mar any wood finish it drips onto; wipe it away immediately with a damp cloth, let the area dry, and sand it.

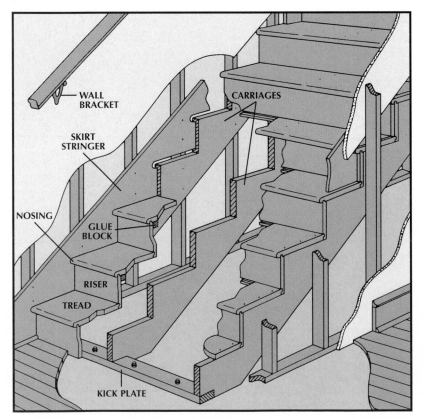

A carriage-supported stairway.
In most older stairways and in a few newer ones, thick sawtooth-notched boards called carriages *(left)* support the treads and provide surfaces for nailing the risers, the vertical boards between treads.

At the bottom, the carriages fit over a kick plate nailed to the floor to keep them from sliding. Each tread has a tongue on its back edge that fits into a groove in the riser behind it and a groove under the front edge that drops over a tongue on the riser below. The treads are also nailed to the carriages. Each tread projects beyond the riser beneath it and ends in a rounded edge called a nosing. Glue blocks are used to reinforce the joints between the treads and risers, and nails through the back of the riser into the tread strengthen that joint.

In this example, the stairway is enclosed by walls on both sides; wall brackets support handrails. Where the stairway meets the wall, a baseboard of finish softwood called a skirt stringer, carefully sawed to fit against the treads and risers, covers and hides their ends.

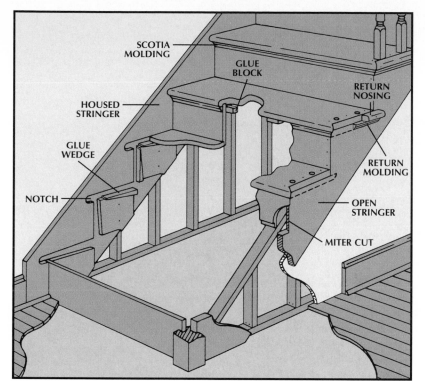

A prefabricated stairway.

In the modern prefabricated stairway, the functions of the carriage and the skirt stringer are combined in one board, the housed stringer. Glue wedges clamp the ends of the treads and risers in V-shaped notches, which are routed into the side of the housed stringer. The treads and risers usually meet in rabbet joints and are glue blocked and nailed.

A walled stairway would use housed stringers on both sides, but an open-sided stairway like the one at left supports the outer ends of the treads on an open stringer cut like a carriage. Since it is too light to serve as a true carriage, the studding of the wall beneath it must be used to provide extra support.

The vertical cuts on the open stringer are mitered to match a miter at the end of the riser, concealing the end grain. The end of each tread has a return nosing nailed on, also hiding end grain. A return molding at the end and a scotia molding at the front complete the tread trim.

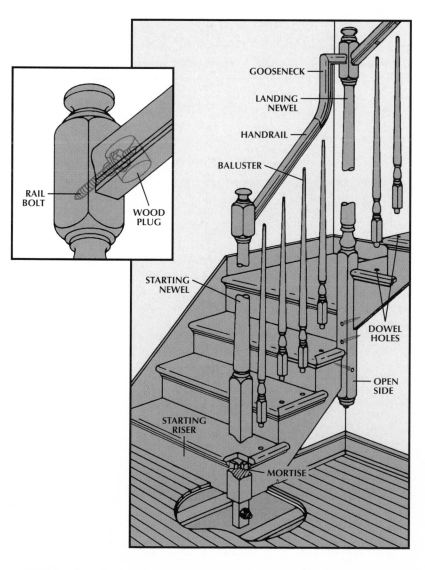

The parts of a balustrade.

Newel posts provide structural support for the railing. At its base the starting newel has slots called mortises to receive the ends of the starting riser and the open stringer. The newel sometimes extends through the floor to be bolted to a joist. Landing newels, also mortised, are bolted to the header joists (pages 95-96) behind them.

The railing is joined to the newels with rail bolts (inset). The lag-bolt end is screwed into the newel post, and the machine-screw end runs into a hole in the end of the railing. A washer and a nut are attached to the machine screw through an access hole bored from underneath the rail. Then the hole is plugged. Some railings rise to the upper newel in a curved piece called a gooseneck.

Vertical balusters are installed between treads and the railing, usually with dowels. Often the tops of the dowels are press-fitted into their holes to keep glue from dripping down the balusters.

In an adaptation of a traditional form, many stairways use a longer starting tread, called a bullnose, and a spiraled railing end called a volute (pages 90-99).

Squeaks, a common problem in older, carriage-supported stairways *(page 64)*, are caused by treads that have separated slightly from the carriage or by the riser's rubbing against other stair parts when stepped on. You can stop the squeak by making the separated portion stay down or by inserting a thin wedge as a shim underneath it.

The repairs described on these pages will also work on modern prefabricated stairways *(page 65)* with housed stringers, though they develop squeaks far less frequently. A special technique for replacing a glue wedge that has worked loose from the tread and housed stringer is shown on page 68.

Locating the Squeak: Use a carpenter's level to find warps, twists, or bows in the treads. While a helper climbs the stairs, listen, watch for rise and fall, and—resting your hand on the tread—feel for vibration.

If the tread spring is minimal, you can eliminate it with angled nails *(below)* or trim head screws. If the tread movement is substantial, use wedges *(opposite, top)*.

Such repairs from the top are usually sufficient. But if you can get to the stairway from underneath you can make a sound and simple fix, preferable because it is invisible, by adding glue blocks to the joint between the tread and the riser, the most common source of squeaks. If the tread is badly warped or humped in the center, rejoin it with a screw through the carriage *(page 68)*.

TOOLS

Carpenter's level
Electric drill with
  bits ($\frac{1}{8}$", $\frac{1}{4}$", $\frac{3}{32}$")
Hammer

Nail set
Utility knife
Screwdriver
Putty knife
Chisel

MATERIALS

Finishing nails ($2\frac{1}{2}$")
Wood putty
Trim head screws
  ($2\frac{1}{2}$")
Hardwood wedges

Glue
Common nails (2")
Construction
  adhesive
Wood screws
  (3" No. 12)

SAFETY TIPS

Goggles protect your eyes from dust and flying debris while you are hammering, chiseling, or drilling.

WORKING FROM ABOVE

Nailing the tread down.
◆ With a helper standing on the tread, drill $\frac{3}{32}$-inch pilot holes angled through the tread and into the riser at the point of movement. If the squeak comes from the ends of the tread, angle the holes into the carriage.
◆ Drive $2\frac{1}{2}$-inch finishing nails into the holes, sink the heads with a nail set, and fill with wood putty.

If the tread spring is too great for nails to close, drill pilot holes as above and secure the tread with $2\frac{1}{2}$-inch trim head screws. Apply paraffin wax to the threads to make the screws turn easily in oak. Countersink the heads and fill the holes with wood putty.

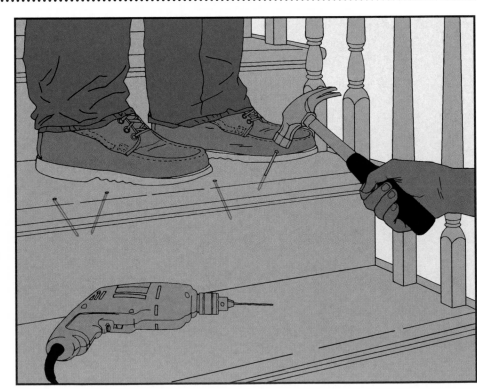

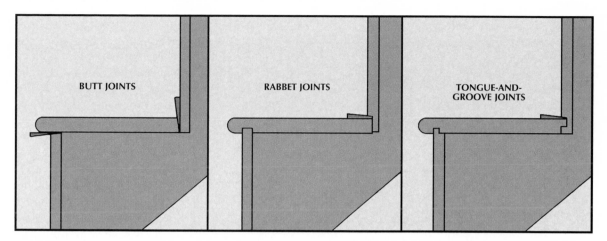

Wedging treads tight.

◆ Remove the scotia molding under the tread nose and insert a knife into the tread joints in order to discover the kind of joints that were used. With butt joints, the knife will slip vertically into the joint behind the tread and horizontally under the tread; with rabbet or tongue-and-groove joints, the knife-entry directions are reversed.

◆ Drive sharply tapered hardwood wedges coated with glue into the cracks as far as possible in the indicated directions.

◆ Cut off the wedges' protruding ends with a utility knife; replace the scotia molding. Use shoe molding to cover joints at the back of the treads.

WORKING FROM BELOW

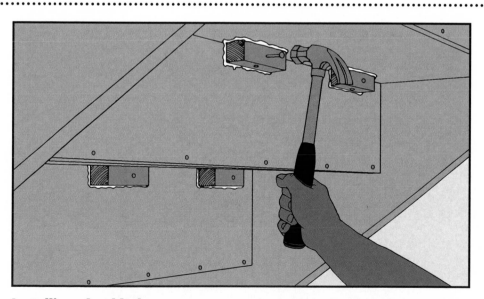

Installing glue blocks.

◆ If the joint has old blocks that have come partly unstuck, pry them off with a screwdriver or putty knife and scrape the dried glue off the tread and riser.

◆ Spread glue on two sides of a block of wood $1\frac{1}{2}$ inches square and about 3 inches long. Press the block into the joint between the tread and the riser and slide it back and forth a little to strengthen the glue bond.

◆ Then fasten the block with a 2-inch common nail in each direction. Add two or three more blocks to each joint.

Drilling through the carriage.

◆ About 2 inches below the tread, chisel a shallow notch into the carriage. With a helper standing on the tread, drill a $\frac{1}{8}$-inch pilot hole angled at about 30 degrees through the notch and $\frac{3}{4}$ inch into the tread *(left)*. Then enlarge the hole through the carriage with a $\frac{1}{4}$-inch bit.

◆ With the helper off the tread, spread a bead of construction adhesive along both sides of the joint between the tread and the carriage, and work it into the joint with a putty knife.

◆ Have the helper stand on the tread again and install a No. 12 wood screw 3 inches long.

RE-SHIMMING A PREFAB STAIRWAY

Replacing loose wedges.

◆ Split out the old wedge with a chisel *(below)*, and pare dried glue and splinters from the notch.

◆ Plane a new wedge from a piece of hardwood to fit within an inch of the riser. Coat the notch, the bottom of the tread, and the top and bottom of the wedge with glue.

◆ Hammer the wedge snugly into the notch, tap it along the side to force it against the notch face, then hit the end a few more times to jam the wedge tightly under the tread.

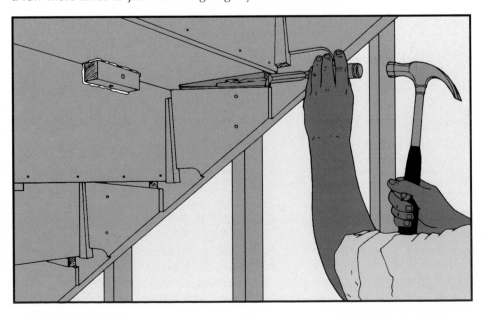

Repairing a Balustrade

The stairway balustrade is an elegant piece of carpentry that is also essential for safety. A broken baluster or a shaky railing should be fixed without delay, in order to preserve both the balustrade's appearance and its stability.

Three Types of Baluster: Tighten a loose baluster with glue, nails, or small wedges; but if it is cracked, dented, or badly scraped, replace it. First, determine how your balusters are fastened. Square-topped balusters usually fit into a shallow groove in the railing. Blocks of wood called fillets are nailed into the grooves between balusters. Sometimes balusters also end at the bottom in the groove of a lower rail, called a buttress cap, that lies on top of a stringer nailed to the ends of the treads and risers *(page 71)*.

Balusters with cylindrical tops fit into holes in the railing. If they do not overlap the return nosing, balusters are also doweled at the bottom, even though a square section may abut the treads. Balusters that overlap the return nosing are probably joined to the tread by a dovetail joint, and you will have to remove the return nosing to make the replacement.

Obtaining a New Baluster: Save the broken baluster as a pattern for a new one. If you cannot match it, have a cabinetmaker turn one. Instead of cutting a dovetail, pin a doweled baluster into the dovetailed tread with a nail *(page 70)*.

Cures for a Shaky Railing: The cause of a wobbly railing is usually a loose starting newel post. For a post in a bullnose tread, run a lag screw up through the floor into the foot of the post. Where there is no bullnose, the solution is to drive a lag screw through the newel and into the boards behind it *(page 71)*.

 **TOOLS**

Compass saw or keyhole saw
Pipe wrench
Electric drill with bits ($\frac{7}{32}$", $\frac{5}{16}$")
Spade bit
Folding rule
Chisel
Pry bar
Forstner bit ($\frac{3}{4}$")
Hammer
Miter box
Socket wrench

 **MATERIALS**

Glue
Finishing nails ($1\frac{1}{2}$")
Lag screws ($\frac{5}{16}$" x 3" and 4") and washers
Scrap wood for pry block
Putty
Scrap 2 x 4 lumber for gauge block

SAFETY TIPS

Protect your eyes with safety goggles when you are hammering nails, using a hammer and chisel, drilling at or above waist level, or levering wood with a pry bar.

REPLACING A DOWELED BALUSTER

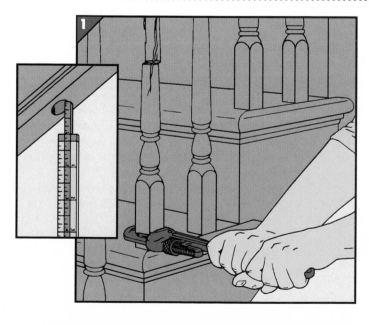

1. Removing the damaged baluster.
◆ Saw the baluster in two and sharply twist the bottom piece with a pipe wrench to break the glue joint at the base *(left)*. Then remove the top piece; if it is stuck, use the wrench.
◆ If the joints do not break, saw the baluster flush, using cardboard on the tread to guard it from the saw. Then drill out the dowel ends with spade bits the size of the dowels on the new baluster.
◆ Trim the bottom dowel to a $\frac{3}{16}$-inch stub.
◆ With a folding rule, measure from the high edge of the dowel hole in the railing to the tread *(inset)* and add $\frac{7}{16}$ inch. Cut off the top dowel to shorten the new baluster to this length.

2. Installing the new baluster.

◆ Smear glue in the tread hole, angle the top dowel into the railing hole, and pull the bottom of the baluster across the tread, lifting the railing about $\frac{1}{4}$ inch.

◆ Seat the bottom dowel in the tread hole. If the railing will not lift, bevel the top dowel where it binds against the side of the hole.

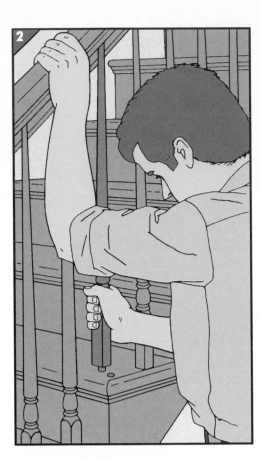

DEALING WITH A DOVETAILED BALUSTER

1. Removing the return nosing.

◆ Use a chisel to crack the joints.

◆ While protecting the stringer with a pry block, insert a pry bar and remove the return molding and return nosing (below).

◆ Saw through the old baluster and hammer it out of the dovetail.

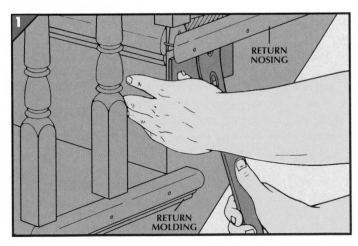

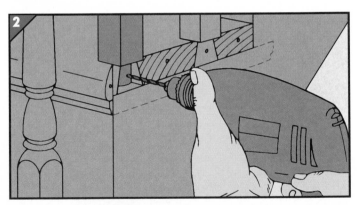

2. Securing the new baluster.

◆ Insert the top of a cut-to-length doweled baluster into the railing hole and set its base in the tread dovetail. Shim behind the dowel, if necessary, to align it with its neighbors.

◆ Drill a $\frac{1}{16}$-inch pilot hole through the dowel into the tread, and drive a $1\frac{1}{2}$-inch finishing nail through the hole into the tread.

◆ Renail the return nosing and return molding through the old holes; putty over the nailheads.

A NEW FILLETED BALUSTER

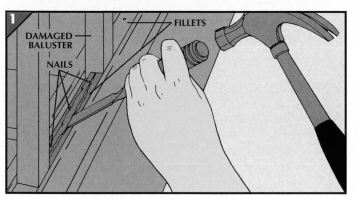

1. Taking out the old baluster.
◆ With a chisel, remove the fillet in the buttress cap on the downstairs side of the damaged baluster *(above)*. Then chisel out the railing fillet on the upstairs side of the baluster.
◆ Hammer each end of the baluster toward the chiseled-out fillet grooves to remove the baluster. Pull any nails left behind and scrape old glue from the grooves.
◆ Obtain the angle for the new baluster ends and fillets by placing the old baluster on top of the new one. Mark the angle on the new baluster and saw it to length.

2. Fastening the new baluster.
◆ Set the baluster against the existing fillets and toenail it to the railing and buttress cap with two $1\frac{1}{2}$-inch finishing nails through each end. Start the nails where the new fillets will hide them, and set the heads.
◆ Measure the length of each new fillet, mark the angle cuts using the old baluster, and cut with a miter box.
◆ Coat the backs with glue and fasten them in the railing and buttress-cap grooves with $1\frac{1}{2}$-inch finishing nails.

TIGHTENING A SHAKY NEWEL

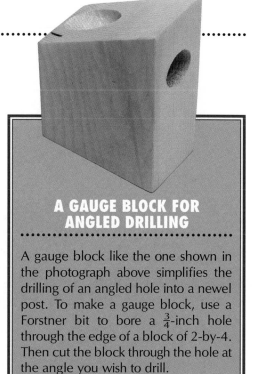

Installing a lag screw.
◆ Hold a gauge block *(box, right)* against the newel, 4 inches from the floor, the hole centered on the post. Guide a $\frac{3}{4}$-inch Forstner bit through the block, and drill a hole $\frac{3}{4}$ inch deep in the newel *(below, right)*. Extend the hole through the newel with a $\frac{5}{16}$-inch bit and into the carriage with a $\frac{7}{32}$-inch bit.
◆ With a socket wrench, drive a $\frac{5}{16}$-inch lag screw 4 inches long fitted with a washer *(overhead view, inset)*. Plug the hole with a dowel, then cut it flush.

To steady a newel set in a bullnose tread, drive two nails through the flooring near the newel. From beneath, measure from the nails to locate the center of the newel dowel. Drill shank and pilot holes and install a $\frac{5}{16}$-inch lag screw 3 inches long. Pull the nails and putty the holes.

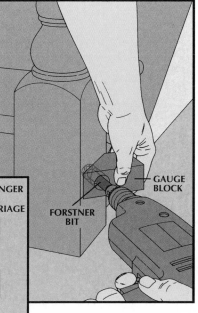

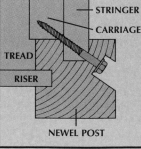

A GAUGE BLOCK FOR ANGLED DRILLING

A gauge block like the one shown in the photograph above simplifies the drilling of an angled hole into a newel post. To make a gauge block, use a Forstner bit to bore a $\frac{3}{4}$-inch hole through the edge of a block of 2-by-4. Then cut the block through the hole at the angle you wish to drill.

Retreading a Stairway

Subject to heavy traffic, stair treads suffer scratches, scrapes, dents, and stains, and may wear unevenly or split. In any type of stairway, you can readily replace individual stair treads with standard lumberyard oak stair tread, which has a nosing milled onto the front edge.

Before removing the old tread *(below)*, study the anatomy drawings on pages 64 and 65 to get a clear picture of how your stairway and balustrade are constructed. For a carriage-supported stairway that has one side open, follow the steps that begin on the page at right. For such a stairway closed on both sides, see page 75.

Replacing Treads on a Prefab Stairway: You can replace a tread set in a housed stringer by chiseling out the wedges beneath the tread *(page 68)* and behind the riser above it, removing both parts, and inserting a new tread and the old riser. If one end of the tread rests on an open stringer, as shown at the top of page 65, remove the balusters *(pages 69-71);* then, from beneath the stairway, hammer first the tread and then the riser free from their nailings.

 TOOLS

Electric drill with
  bits ($\frac{3}{4}$", $\frac{3}{32}$")
Compass saw or
  keyhole saw
Hammer
Chisel

Plumb bob
Combination square
Backsaw
Block plane
Backsaw
Coping saw
Caulk gun
Nail set

 **MATERIALS**

Oak stair tread
  ($1\frac{1}{16}$" thick and
  $11\frac{1}{2}$" wide)

Construction
  adhesive
Finishing nails ($2\frac{1}{2}$")
Wood putty
Glue

 **SAFETY TIPS**

When hammering or chiseling, wear safety goggles to protect your eyes from flying debris or loose nails.

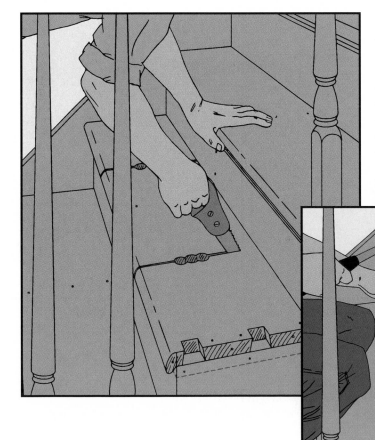

Removing the old tread.

◆ Take off the balusters *(pages 69-71)* and moldings, then drill starting holes for a compass saw or keyhole saw.

◆ Cut across the tread in two places *(left)* up to the edges of the risers in front and behind; stop the cut before damaging their exposed surfaces.

◆ Drive a chisel into the middle third of the tread over the front riser *(inset)* so that the nosing breaks off without damaging the riser tongue. Working toward the back riser, split off pieces of tread, prying the last inch or so gently away from the nails holding it to the back riser.

◆ Hammer the chisel sideways into the ends of the remaining tread, splitting around nails. Pull out the pieces; cut off all protruding nails.

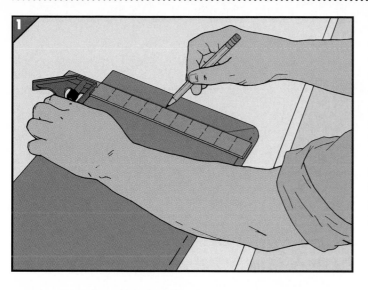

1. Laying out the nosing cuts.
◆ First saw the new tread to length to fit under the skirt stringer and flush with the outer edge of the outside carriage.
◆ In trimming the tread to width, allow for rabbet or tongue-and-groove joints between treads and risers *(page 67)*. Rout the appropriate joints on the tread, or have a mill do it.
◆ With a combination square, mark the cuts for the return nosing on the outside end of the new tread *(left)*. Draw a 45-degree line in from the front corner of the tread for the miter cut, then mark a crosscut the width of the nosing.

2. Sawing the cuts.
Cut along the 45-degree line with a backsaw *(left)*, then crosscut along the mark with a keyhole saw held against a 1-by-2 guide clamped to the tread. Smooth the cuts with a block plane and a chisel.

3. Laying out dovetail mortises.
◆ With the tread temporarily in place, use a plumb bob to mark the point on the tread directly beneath the center of a railing hole.
◆ Angle the upper end of the baluster into the hole, hold the bottom against the tread end centered on the plumb-bob mark, and scribe the dovetail angles.
◆ With a combination square, extend the lines onto the top and bottom of the tread, and connect them with lines as far in as the thickness of the dovetail. Repeat for the other baluster.

If the balusters are doweled into the treads, use the plumb-bob mark as the center for dowel holes in the new tread. With a spade bit, drill holes of the dowel diameter $\frac{3}{8}$ inch deep.

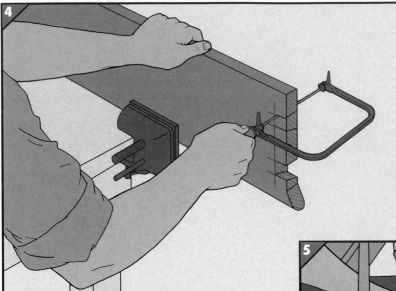

4. Sawing out the dovetails.

Cut the sides of the dovetails just inside the marks with a backsaw, then cut the back with a coping saw *(left)*. Smooth the saw cuts by gently paring them with a chisel.

5. Gluing down the new tread.

◆ Mark the tread with a pencil or piece of chalk at the points where it will lie over the carriages, then drill three $\frac{3}{32}$-inch pilot holes across the tread at each point.

◆ Spread generous beads of construction adhesive along the tops of the carriages *(right)*. Slide the tread into place under the skirt stringer. Drive $2\frac{1}{2}$-inch finishing nails through the pilot holes into the carriages, countersink the heads with a nail set, and fill the holes with wood putty. Keep traffic off the tread for 3 hours to let the adhesive set. Replace the balusters, the return nosing, and the moldings, as shown on pages 70 to 71.

6. Fastening from underneath.

If you can reach the underside of the stairway, drill $\frac{3}{32}$-inch pilot holes through the riser into the tread and drive $2\frac{1}{2}$-inch nails. Use glue blocks *(page 67)* along the joint between the tread and the riser below.

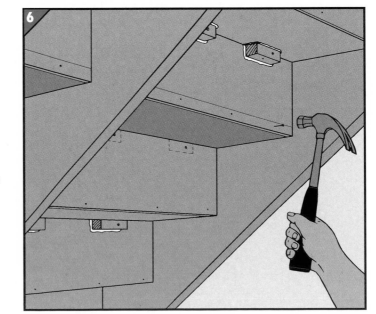

LAYING A NEW TREAD ON A CLOSED STAIR

1. Finding the length of the new tread.

Measure from the face of one skirt stringer across the stairway into the notch beneath the other *(right)*. Subtract $\frac{1}{8}$ inch to leave some play, and cut the new tread to this length. If the front riser was tongued or rabbeted into the old tread, chisel and plane it flush with the carriages.

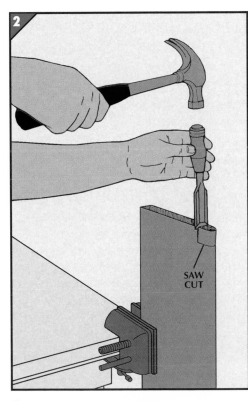

2. Notching the nosing.

Using a backsaw and a chisel, make a notch in one of the front corners of the new tread. The distance from the end of the tread to the saw cut should be equal to the depth of the slot under the skirt stringer; the chisel split should be made as far back from the nosing as the amount of overhang of the tread above, plus $\frac{1}{2}$ inch for play. Save the cutout scrap of nosing to use in Step 3.

3. Installing the tread.

◆ Apply construction adhesive to the tops of the carriages.
◆ Holding the uncut end of the tread angled upward, insert the notched end beneath the skirt stringer *(above)*. The notch will allow you to pull the tread far enough forward to avoid hitting the nose of the tread above.
◆ Lower the other end to the carriages, push the tread tight against the back riser, then slide it sideways until the tread notch is revealed.
◆ Glue and nail the scrap of nosing into the tread notch. Drill pilot holes, nail the tread down, toenailing into the outer carriages if they are under the stringers. Then set the heads and fill the holes with wood putty.

75

Consider adding a stairway if the only way to reach your basement is through an exterior door, or if you can get to your attic only by balancing on a chair. But before you can install one, you must create in the upper floor an access hole reinforced with new framing to do the work of the joists you cut out to make the opening.

Planning the Work: Locate the stairs so that existing walls will not have to be removed or shifted; to simplify framing, make the longer sides of the opening run parallel to the joists (*opposite*). Leave at least 3 feet between the top or bottom treads and a facing wall to provide turning space.

Consult local building codes to get minimum dimensions for the space between the handrails and for headroom. Some codes stipulate that main stairs have at least 32 inches between the handrails, even more if its sides are finished with wood or wallboard. Stair openings must be long enough so you don't bump your head as you descend. Most codes require a minimum of 76 inches for basement stairs and 80 inches for main stairs.

How to measure and mark the opening depends on the type of stairway to be installed. For most kinds, follow the procedure for a cleat basement stairway (*page 86*); measuring instructions for two exceptions, a spiral staircase and a disappearing stairway, are on page 80. All openings are cut and reinforced as described here and opposite, regardless of stairway type.

Temporary Support: Before cutting into the ceiling, install shoring. Doing so is particularly important for an opening that runs perpendicular to joists, where as many as six joists may have to be cut for a conventional stair. In this case, permanent posts or walls must be erected as supports for the severed joists, called tail joists.

For a spiral-stairway opening, wallboard and moldings must be installed before the stair; in most other instances, finish work follows stair installation. Use scraps of ceiling material to patch gaps around the stair opening. Special molding called landing nosing can be put in around the upper edges of the opening if there will be a balustrade. Otherwise, hide the exposed plaster, plywood, and finish flooring with decorative moldings.

⚠️ **CAUTION** *Before cutting into your floor, read the asbestos warning on page 34.*

 TOOLS

Hammer
Handsaw
Electric drill
Chalk line
Circular saw
Pry bar

 **MATERIALS**

2 x 4s
2 x 10s
4 x 4s

Common nails
 (3" and $3\frac{1}{2}$")
Plywood ($\frac{1}{2}$" and $\frac{5}{8}$")
Joist hangers, single
 and double
Framing connectors

 **SAFETY TIPS**

Protect your eyes from dust and flying debris while you are hammering or sawing by wearing safety goggles. Earplugs reduce the noise of a circular saw to a safe level, and wearing a hard hat is advisable when handling heavy objects overhead or working close to joists overhead.

⚠️ **CAUTION**

Truss Joists

Inspect your joists before cutting a stair opening. If they look like the one shown here, called a truss or open-web joist, do not cut them without advice from a structural engineer.

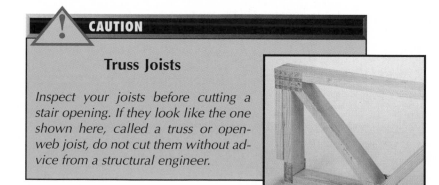

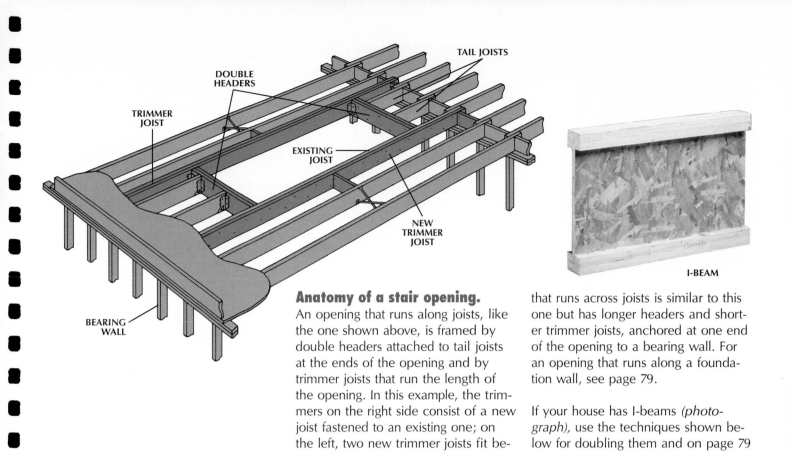

TAIL JOISTS

DOUBLE HEADERS

TRIMMER JOIST

EXISTING JOIST

NEW TRIMMER JOIST

BEARING WALL

I-BEAM

Anatomy of a stair opening.
An opening that runs along joists, like the one shown above, is framed by double headers attached to tail joists at the ends of the opening and by trimmer joists that run the length of the opening. In this example, the trimmers on the right side consist of a new joist fastened to an existing one; on the left, two new trimmer joists fit between existing floor joists. An opening that runs across joists is similar to this one but has longer headers and shorter trimmer joists, anchored at one end of the opening to a bearing wall. For an opening that runs along a foundation wall, see page 79.

If your house has I-beams *(photograph),* use the techniques shown below for doubling them and on page 79 for hanging headers from them.

MAKING AN OPENING

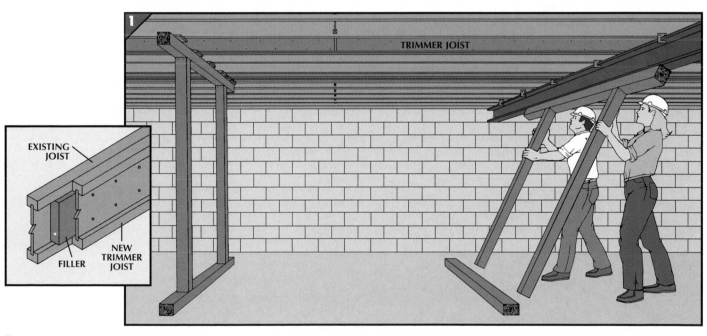

1

TRIMMER JOIST

EXISTING JOIST

FILLER

NEW TRIMMER JOIST

1. Supporting the floor.
◆ Mark the opening as shown on page 87, Step 1, then mark its dimensions on the subfloor. Drill a hole up through the floor at each corner.
◆ Install trimmer joists on each side of the proposed opening *(page 16),* using triple trimmers to bear the weight of a partition wall above. To double I-beams, install lumber in the void between them *(inset)* so that the filler extends 1 foot to both sides of header attachment points. Hammer ten 3-inch nails through one joist, the filler, and the second joist; bend exposed nail points to clinch them.
◆ Install the shoring *(pages 22-24)* beyond each end of the opening.

2. Cutting the opening.

◆ On the upper floor, find the holes drilled at the corners of the planned stair opening, extend the opening's length 3 inches on each end to allow for the thickness of the double headers *(Step 5),* and snap four chalk lines to mark the opening boundaries.

◆ Saw through the finish floor and subfloor along the two sides of the opening that cross the floorboards at right angles.

◆ Pry up the cut boards as shown on page 12. Then saw through the subfloor along the other two sides.

3. Removing the subfloor.

◆ To loosen the subfloor from the joists, pound upward with a 2-by-4 along the sides of each joist under the sawed section.

◆ Then use a pry bar from above to remove the material.

4. Cutting the joists.

◆ Hand-saw the joists flush with the opening while a helper supports each joist from below to prevent it from pinching the saw as you cut.

◆ From the joist sections thus removed, cut four lengths to fit between the trimmer joists at each end of the opening. Fasten them together in pairs with 3-inch nails in a W pattern to serve as headers.

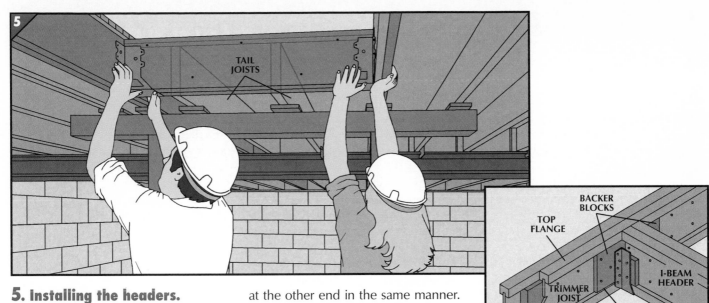

5. Installing the headers.

◆ For lumber joists, nail 3-inch single joist hangers to each end of a double header. Butt the header side against the ends of the tail joists as shown above.

◆ Nail the joist hangers to the trimmer joists using all nail holes in the hangers.

◆ Nail 1½-inch hangers onto the tail joists and the headers from below.

◆ Then mount the other double header

at the other end in the same manner.

◆ For I-beams, make a double header using the doubling method in Step 1. Install a backer block at each trimmer attachment point *(inset)*. Fit the backer against the trimmer joist's top flange, but leave a gap no wider than ⅛ inch at the bottom flange, to keep weight off of it.

◆ To the ends of the headers, nail a

double joist hanger, filling in any gaps between hanger and header with wood block.

◆ Nail the hanger to the trimmer joist.

◆ Connect the header to the tail joists with single joist hangers.

A VARIATION FOR A FOUNDATION WALL

Setting headers on the wall.

◆ If you are installing a basement stair alongside a masonry wall, first install a trimmer joist *(right)*.

◆ Then put the headers—without joist hangers—against the the cut tail joists, and between the trimmer and the stringer.

◆ Fasten the headers to the trimmer and tail joists as shown in Step 5.

◆ Cut a support board to fit between the headers, and nail it to the stringer.

◆ Use metal framing connectors to fasten the headers to the stringer joist and support board.

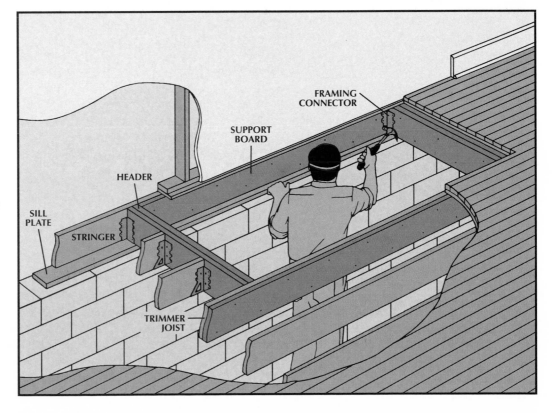

Many homes lack the space for a full flight of stairs to an attic or an additional flight between main floors. But even the most cramped floor plans can accommodate the two stairways shown on these pages.

A disappearing stair, concealed behind a plywood panel, pulls down to provide access to attic storage space, then folds back into the ceiling when not in use. A spiral stairway of hardwood, aluminum, or steel not only adds style and beauty to any room, but also takes 70 percent less space than a regular stairway. Both types require a stairwell opening *(pages 76-79)* cut to the dimensions specified by the manufacturer.

Choosing a Disappearing Stairway: Preassembled folding attic stairs come in standard sizes to fit openings 25 to 30 inches wide and 54 to 60 inches long. If you make the opening parallel to the ceiling joists, you need cut only one joist to accommodate the stair; if you must cross the joists, you may have to cut as many as three framing members.

Before ordering, measure the ceiling height and check the clearance and attic headroom required for the model you have chosen. Clearance—the amount of space needed to unfold the stairs—is measured hori-

zontally on the floor directly beneath the opening. Headroom is the free space needed above the ceiling for the supporting hardware and the handrail.

Measuring for a Spiral Stairway: First, determine the location and stair diameter best suited to your floor plan. Find the most comfortable direction of entry and exit to and from the stairway on both floors and decide whether you prefer a right-hand (counterclockwise) or a left-hand stair. Spiral stairs are available as kits; you can choose a full spiral or a three-quarter turn.

When ordering a spiral stairway, you must specify the exact height of the stair from finished floor to finished floor. To get an accurate measurement, drill a $\frac{1}{8}$-inch hole through the upper floor and drop a plumb bob to the floor below. The manufacturer can then help you determine the number and size of the treads. The stair kit will include all the hardware and any specialized tools, such as a hex key, you will need.

Before installation, mark the location of each tread on the center pole. Counting the landing as one tread, divide the floor-to-floor height in inches by the number of treads in the kit, then space the marks equidistantly along the center pole.

 TOOLS

Electric drill with $\frac{3}{8}$" bit
Yardstick
Handsaw
Plumb bob
Ratchet wrench
Carpenter's level

 **MATERIALS**

Bolts ($\frac{3}{8}$" x $4\frac{1}{2}$")
Sandpaper
Braces (2 x 4)

 **SAFETY TIPS**

To protect your eyes, wear safety goggles when drilling or sawing at or above the level of your waist.

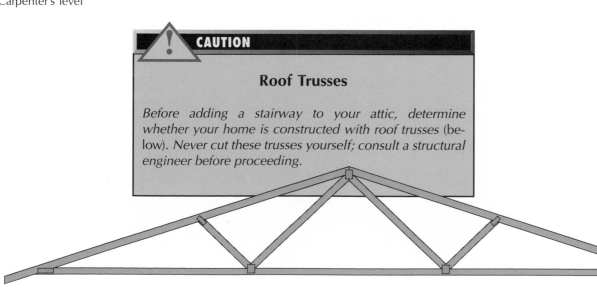

⚠ CAUTION

Roof Trusses

Before adding a stairway to your attic, determine whether your home is constructed with roof trusses (below). Never cut these trusses yourself; consult a structural engineer before proceeding.

INSTALLING A DISAPPEARING STAIR

1. Attaching the stair.

After cutting and framing the opening, bolt the stair's frame to the joists and headers with $\frac{3}{8}$- by $4\frac{1}{2}$-inch bolts. To hold it in place while drilling holes and inserting bolts, shim it level on top of two 2-by-4 braces fastened to the double joists by nails driven through the ceiling and removed after the stair is installed.

2 x 4 BRACE

SIDE RAIL

CUTTING LINE

2. Cutting the side rails to size.

◆ Pull the stair from the stair box, unfold the middle section, and, following the angle of the stair, measure the distances from the front and rear edges of this section to the floor.

◆ Mark the side rails of the bottom section with these measurements—be sure not to reverse the distances—and draw cutting lines, indicated here by a broken line, between the marks. Saw along the lines on each side rail, and smooth the cuts with sandpaper.

A STAIRWAY WITH A TWIST

Anatomy of a spiral stair.
This typical metal staircase consists of a center pole mounted on a base plate and twelve treads secured to the post and braced at their outer edges by twelve balusters. A landing plate and a landing rail top the stairs; a starting post at the bottom forms the starting point for a curving flexible handrail screwed to the balusters.

To strengthen the floor on which the stair will rest, double the joists beneath the center pole *(page 76)*. If the center pole falls between joists, double the joists on either side and insert wood spacing blocks *(page 17, Step 1)* between the doubled joists to provide reinforcement.

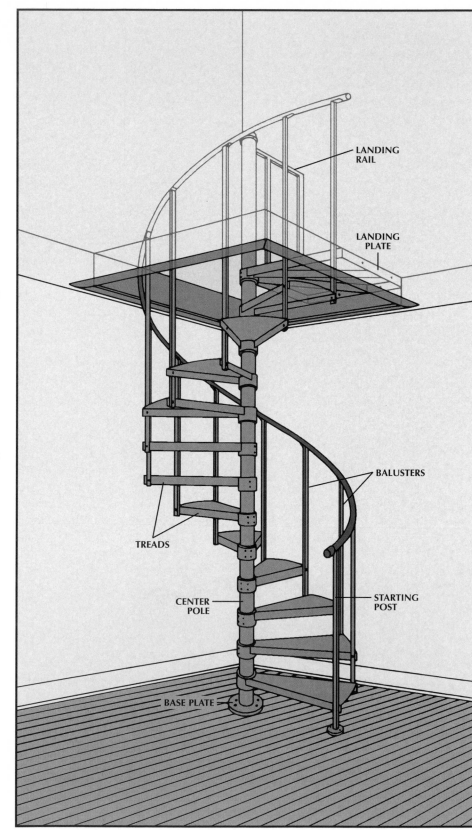

LANDING RAIL

LANDING PLATE

BALUSTERS

TREADS

CENTER POLE

STARTING POST

BASE PLATE

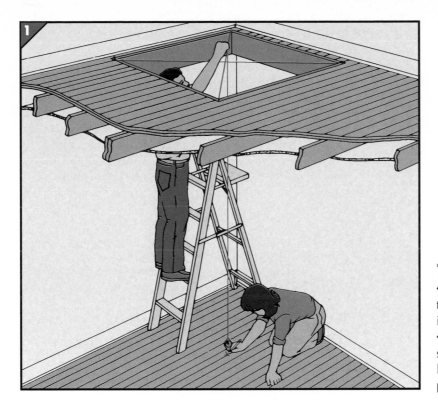

1. Positioning the center pole.
◆ Stretch two strings diagonally across the stairway opening from nails driven into the corners.
◆ Drop a plumb line from the intersection of the strings to the floor below, and then mark the spot where the plumb bob touches the floor.

2. Securing the pole.
◆ Stand the center pole on the floor mark; make sure it is both centered and plumb.
◆ Using the predrilled holes in the base plate as a guide *(right),* drill pilot holes into the subflooring for the lag bolts provided with the kit. On a concrete floor, drill the holes with a masonry bit and insert expansion anchors for the lag bolts.
◆ Then slide all the treads, faceup, to the bottom of the center pole.

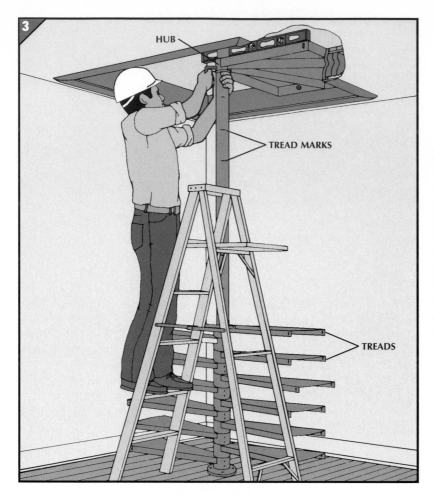

3. Installing the landing plate.

◆ Align the landing plate with the top tread mark. While a helper levels the plate, insert the four setscrews into the hub and, with the kit's hex key, tighten them loosely against the center pole.

◆ Drill pilot holes through the landing-plate flanges into a joist and header of the hole framing, and fasten the landing plate to the framing with lag bolts. Make a final leveling adjustment, then tighten the setscrews *(left)*.

4. Bolting the top baluster.

Align the upper hole of a baluster with the predrilled hole in the landing-plate flange. Then use a ratchet wrench to fasten the baluster to the landing plate with a nut, bolt, and washer furnished with the kit *(inset)*.

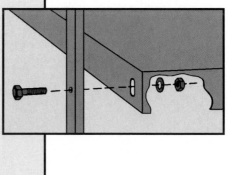

5. Attaching the treads.

◆ Align the top tread with the top tread mark, and the hole at the back of this tread with the open hole in the installed baluster; level the tread and bolt it to the baluster, as in Step 4.

◆ Tighten the four setscrews in the tread hub. Repeat the procedure down to the floor, fastening each tread to the one below it with the balusters.

◆ At the base of the stair, bolt the starting post to the bottom tread and secure the post to the floor with lag bolts, as in Step 2.

6. Installing the handrail.

◆ Set the plastic handrail over the starting post and the bottom baluster, leaving a 2-inch overhang beyond the post. Then, using the predrilled flanges on the starting post and baluster as guides *(inset)*, drill pilot holes into the underside of the handrail *(left)*.

◆ Fasten the rail to both the post and baluster with the self-tapping screws that are in the kit. Proceed up the stair, unwinding the rail as you go and drilling pilot holes at each baluster. Allow a 2-inch overhang beyond the top baluster and cut off the excess rail. Install the caps that come with the kit over the ends of the handrail and the top of the center pole.

◆ Then bolt the landing rail to the landing plate and the center pole.

Simple Stairs for the Basement

You can create a new entrance to a basement with a simple but sturdy cleat stairway built from scratch. There are no carriages or risers; instead, the treads rest on small blocks, or cleats, attached to the inside faces of 2-by-10 support boards.

The supports are fastened to the stairwell header with steel framing connectors and either braced with 2-by-4 posts or nailed to an adjacent wall. A 2-by-4 kick plate *(page 89, Step 2)* secures the bottom of the supports to the concrete floor.

The Need for Proper Planning: For comfort and safety, any stairway must maintain a precise ratio of vertical and horizontal dimensions, called, respectively, the unit rise and the unit run.

Since basement stairs should not be too steep, carpenters keep the unit rise at around 7 inches and make sure that the sum of the two measurements falls between 17 and 18 inches *(below)*.

Local building codes may impose additional requirements, such as nosings on each tread to give more footroom. You can buy pre-milled tread stock with a rounded nosing on one edge.

The width of the stairway will determine the thickness of the treads—at least $1\frac{1}{16}$ inches for supports up to 30 inches apart, $1\frac{1}{2}$ inches for spans up to 36 inches.

Headroom, measured from the ceiling to the nose of a tread, is also important; generally, building codes specify at least 76 inches for basement stairs.

Handrails for Safety's Sake: Handrails should be 30 to 34 inches above the tread nosings. For rough stairs, they can be simple lengths of 2-by-3. On the open side of a stairway, bolt 2-by-3 posts to the outside of the support, then screw the handrail to the posts and to the inside trimmer joist of the stair opening. On a foundation wall, mount rail brackets with lead anchors, lag screws, and washers.

TOOLS

Tape measure
Plumb bob
Framing square
Electric drill with counterbore
   and masonry bits
Carpenter's level

MATERIALS

Supports (2 x 10)
Tread stock
Cleats (1 x 3)
Kick plate and support posts (2 x 4)
Framing connectors
Lead anchors, lag screws, and washers
Common or masonry nails (3")

SAFETY TIPS

When hammering, wear safety goggles to protect your eyes from flying debris or loose nails.

Establishing the rise and run.
◆ Before cutting an opening in the floor *(pages 76-79)*, you must determine the dimensions of the stairway. First drill a hole through the floor at the spot where you want the top of the stairway, and measure the distance between the upper and lower floors—97 inches in this example. This figure is the total rise of the stairway.
◆ Divide the total rise by 7 to get the number of steps; round fractions up for a shallower stairway, down for a steeper one. Here, the fraction has been rounded down, resulting in 13 steps. Then divide the total rise by 13. The result is $7\frac{6}{13}$, the unit rise.
◆ Since the unit run plus the unit rise should equal 17 to 18 inches, the unit run can be between $9\frac{7}{13}$ and $10\frac{7}{13}$ inches. Pick a middle distance, here 10 inches. There is always one less unit run than unit rise because the top tread is the upper floor, so the total run is 12 times 10 inches—120 inches.

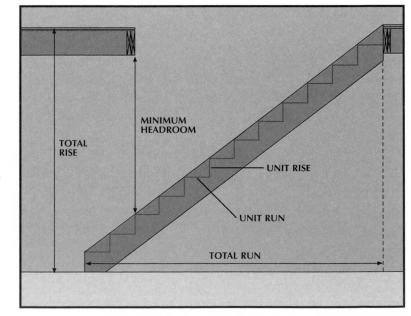

PREPARING TREAD SUPPORTS

1. Marking the stair opening.

◆ Mark the lower floor directly beneath the hole you drilled in the upper floor, then measure and mark the total run on the lower floor.

◆ Extend the total-run mark to the foundation wall and draw the first few unit-run and unit-rise lines on the wall. To the unit-run lines, which indicate the placement of the treads, add the width of the tread nos-ing as specified by your local building codes.

◆ Measure down from the ceiling to the nose of the treads *(left)*. When you reach a tread where the distance is less than the minimum headroom allowed by local building codes, go to the next lower tread mark.

◆ Mark the ceiling directly above the nose of this tread for the downstairs end of the opening. Then cut the stair opening as described on pages 76 to 79.

2. Drawing the floor line.

◆ Place a framing square near one end of a 2-by-10 support board so the unit-run measurement, read on one outer scale, intersects the edge.

◆ Shift the square until the unit rise, read on the outer scale of the other leg, intersects the same edge of the board. As shown here the unit rise is $7\frac{6}{13}$; the unit run is 10 inches. Square gauges *(photo)* attached to the legs of the square at the correct measurements will facilitate marking the board.

◆ Draw a pencil line around the outer edges of the square *(right)*. Then extend the unit-run line across the board to mark the floor line.

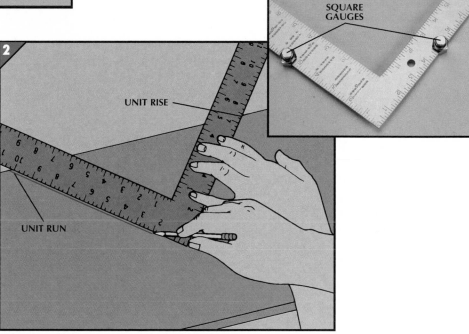

3. Adjusting for a finish floor.

If you plan to add a finish floor to your concrete basement slab *(pages 42-43)*, you must adjust the floor line on the support board to allow for the thickness of the finish floor. Draw a second parallel line closer to the end of the board at a distance equal to the thickness of the finish floor *(left)*.

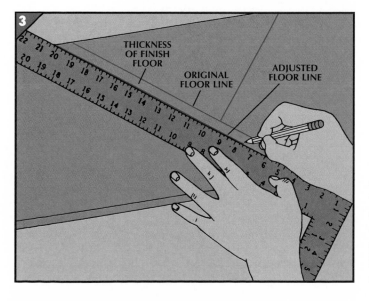

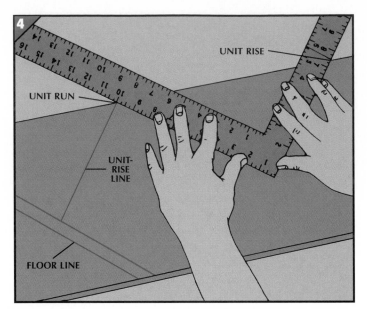

4. Marking unit run and unit rise.

◆ Slide the framing square up the support so that the unit-run measurement on one outer scale hits the end of the first unit-rise line. Make certain the unit-rise measurement on the other leg of the square is also at the edge of the board *(left);* mark around the square.

◆ Repeat the operation, moving the framing square up the board to mark unit-run and unit-rise lines for each step.

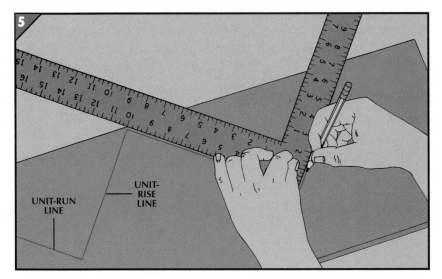

5. Plotting the header line.

◆ At the top of the board, mark the last unit-run and unit-rise lines *(left).* Then extend the topmost unit-rise line down to the lower edge of the board to indicate where the support will meet the stair-opening header.

◆ Cut the support along the adjusted floor line, first unit-rise line, and header line. Then cut a $1\frac{1}{2}$- by $3\frac{1}{2}$-inch notch in the bottom front of the board for the kick plate.

6. Finishing the support.

◆ Draw a parallel line below each unit-run line at a distance equal to the thickness of a tread.

◆ Place the top of a 1-by-3 cleat, cut to the length of the unit run, along each new line except the top one.

◆ Use a counterbore bit for drilling pilot holes, and secure each cleat with five screws.

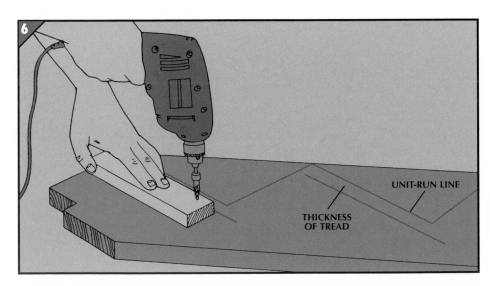

INSTALLING THE SUPPORTS

1. Securing a support to the header.
◆ Temporarily tack the top of the support in place against the stair-opening header. Check to see that the cleats are level, then secure the top of the support with a framing connector *(left)*.
◆ Bend the end of one leg of the connector to fit the bottom of the header *(inset)*. Use a center punch to make additional nail holes in a joist hanger if the framing connector overlaps one at the header.
◆ After the framing connector is in place, screw the top cleat to the up-permost unit-run line on the support.

SUPPORT   BOTTOM OF HEADER

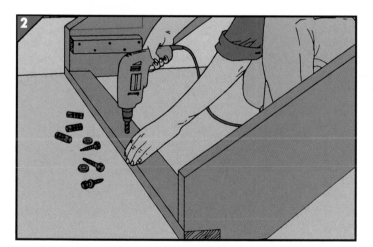

2. Fastening supports to the floor.
◆ Position a 2-by-4 kick plate under the notches in the supports and drill through it to mark the concrete. Then set it aside and use a masonry bit to drill holes for lead anchors.
◆ Replace the plate, fasten it with lag screws and washers, and toenail the supports to it.

3. Bracing the supports.
◆ For a support running along a wall, use 3-inch masonry nails for foundations, or common nails for studs, to secure it.
◆ For an open support, fasten a 2-by-4 plate to the floor beneath the support board with bolts and anchors.
◆ Hold a 2-by-4 plumb on the plate, and mark it for an angle cut along the lower edge of the support *(right)*. Cut the 2-by-4 along this line, then toe-nail it to the plate and the support.
◆ Cut treads to fit between the supports, then nail them in place, angling the nails so that they enter the support boards as well as the cleats.

PLATE   SUPPORT POST

A Prefab Stair and Railing

When replacing a main stairway or creating an attractive passageway to a newly finished basement or attic, you may want something more elaborate than the simple stairs shown on the preceding pages. A handsome but economical solution is a factory-built stairway with a graceful balustrade assembled from stock parts *(page 65)*.

Where to Begin: Ordering the stair correctly is the crucial first step. Some stair companies have local representatives who will help you choose a stair and write the specifications for it, or you can order it yourself *(checklist)*. In either case, it is your responsibility to be sure the installation will comply with local building codes.

A Balustrade for an Open Stair: A stair enclosed by walls simply needs handrails screwed to the wall framing, but any open side of a stairway must have a balustrade. A stud wall underneath provides a finished look, while offering a measure of support to prevent bounce in the stairs. You must also install a railing around the stair opening on the upper floor wherever the opening is not bordered by a wall.

Because of intricate joinery, installing a balustrade is the trickiest, most time-consuming part of the job. A bullnose tread at the bottom of the stairs *(opposite)* simplifies the task since the starting newel is secured to the bullnose without the intricate cuts required for a landing newel *(pages 95-96)*.

Special Parts of the Railing: A common, attractive treatment for the bottom of the handrail is a spiral volute, supported by the starting newel and several balusters *(page 99)*. You can save work by asking the stair company to attach the volute to the rail at the mill.

A gooseneck makes a fluid transition from the railing to the landing newel. Buy a "one-riser" gooseneck *(page 96)* if your code calls for a landing rail 36 inches above the landing finish floor; a higher rail requires a longer, "two-riser" gooseneck.

Making the Job Look Professional: Assembling the balustrade requires precision craftsmanship. To get a good fit, rent, borrow, or buy several specialized woodworking tools. The hole for the starting newel calls for a heavy-duty $\frac{1}{2}$-inch drill and an auger bit that corresponds to the size of either the dowel in the newel post or the insert screwed into a solid bullnose tread. A power miter box is essential for making accurate cuts on the rail and gooseneck, while a router will make landing-newel cuts faster and more accurately than a chisel.

Preparing for the New Stairs: If you are replacing a stairway, have a professional remove the existing one; older stairways, often built into the house framing, may be difficult to detach. Before installing the new stairs, you must prepare the opening in the upper floor *(pages 76-79)*. Doing so may require taking up a portion of the finish flooring. Adapt the procedure shown on page 12, taking care to preserve as many boards as possible for reinstallation.

TOOLS

Electric drill with bits ($\frac{1}{8}$", $\frac{1}{4}$", $\frac{3}{8}$", 1")
Spade bits
Electronic stud finder
Awl
Two combination squares
Level (4')
Adjustable wrench
Hand-screw clamps
Locking pliers
Router with rabbeting bit
Hand saw
Chisel
Framing square
Power miter box
Rubber mallet
Vise
Nail set
Folding rule

MATERIALS

2 x 4s
Shims
Finishing nails ($3\frac{1}{2}$", $2\frac{1}{2}$")
Plywood spacers ($\frac{1}{2}$")
Common nails ($2\frac{1}{2}$")
Sandpaper
Epoxy putty
Carpenter's glue
Round-head wood screws (No. 8)
Trim washers
Lag screws ($\frac{3}{8}$") and washers
Rail bolts ($\frac{3}{8}$")
Wallboard ($\frac{1}{2}$")

SAFETY TIPS

Protect your eyes from flying debris with safety goggles when hammering, sawing, routing, and drilling.

Ordering the Stairs Yourself

✔ Measure the stair's total rise and run *(page 86)*. Check your code for the minimum width.

✔ Know how much of the stair will be enclosed between two walls and how much will not.

✔ Ask for a landing tread to install at the top of the stair.

✔ Order a complete balustrade—gooseneck, volute, newel posts, balusters, and handrail, plus rail bolts *(page 65)* to join railing sections and hardwood plugs to fill any access holes.

✔ Purchase finish molding to conceal joints.

INSTALLING THE STAIRWAY

TOP RISER

HEADER

HOUSED STRINGER

BULLNOSE

1. Positioning the stair.
◆ In the top riser, drill $\frac{1}{8}$" pilot holes for finishing nails spaced 10 inches apart horizontally and 2 inches apart vertically.
◆ Station a helper on the upper floor and, with two other helpers, walk the stair into position. Place the housed stringer against the wall and the top riser against the double header.
◆ Nail two 2-by-4 blocks to the floor at the bottom of the stair to hold it in position temporarily *(left)*.
◆ Shim beneath the bullnose as necessary to bring the treads level and the top riser exactly flush with the surface of the subflooring on the upper floor.

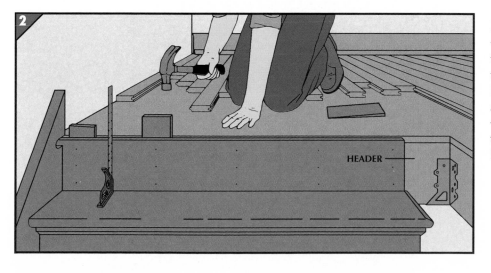

HEADER

2. Fastening the top riser.
◆ Tap wood shims into any gaps between the top riser and the header in the stair opening. Insert the shims behind the pilot holes drilled in Step 1, as shown at left.
◆ Drive a $3\frac{1}{2}$-inch finishing nail through each pilot hole and into the header.

3. Securing the housed stringer.

◆ Using a stud finder, locate and mark the positions of the studs behind the housed stringer.
◆ Drill two $\frac{1}{8}$-inch pilot holes through the stringer into the center of each stud, then fasten the stringer to the studs with $3\frac{1}{2}$-inch finishing nails.

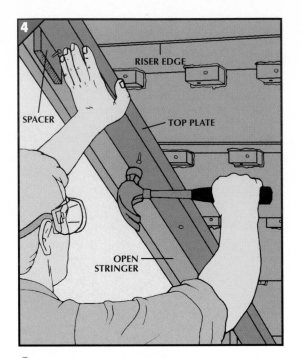

4. Building a stud wall.

◆ Tack spacers of $\frac{1}{2}$-inch plywood to the open stringer, reserving space for wallboard.
◆ With a helper, hold a 2-by-4 against the spacers. At each riser, drive a $2\frac{1}{2}$-inch common nail through the board just far enough to mark the riser edge. Set the board aside and drill a $\frac{1}{8}$-inch pilot hole at each mark.
◆ Reposition the 2-by-4 and nail it in place as a top plate (above).
◆ Nail a sole plate to the floor below the top plate, then miter studs on one end and toenail them to the plates.

ATTACHING A NEWEL TO A HOLLOW BULLNOSE

1. Marking the bullnose.

Cut out the printed paper template supplied by the stair company, and place it on the bullnose tread with its cutout corner fitted to the corner of the riser. Push the tip of an awl through the template and into the tread to mark the centers of the newel post and the bullnose balusters.

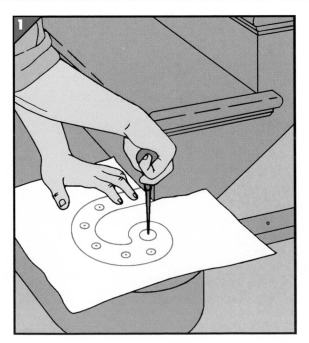

SHELF

2. A hole for the starting newel.

◆ Rent a heavy-duty $\frac{1}{2}$-inch electric drill and an auger bit equal to the diameter of the dowel. Bore a vertical hole through the bullnose tread and the shelves below it. To make sure that the hole is perfectly plumb, have helpers sight the bit against two combination squares *(left)*; drill in short bursts, adjusting the angle of the bit between bursts according to your helpers' instructions.

◆ Slide the dowel protruding from the bottom of the newel into the hole until the base of the newel rests on the tread. If the dowel is too long, trim it; if it is too thick, sand it down to fit.

3. Installing the newel.

◆ Plumb the newel with a 4-foot level. If necessary, enlarge the hole slightly with the auger and place shims between the newel's base and the tread.

◆ Remove the newel and pack about a pint of two-part epoxy putty in the hole with a scrap piece of wood, then set the newel in the hole so that the dowel's end rests in the putty at the bottom.

◆ Hold the newel plumb while a helper nails braces to the newel, the stringer, and the nosing of the second tread with finishing nails *(right)*.

◆ Allow 24 hours for the putty to set.

If you have access to the underside of the subfloor, drive a lag screw fitted with a washer through the subfloor into the end of the dowel *(page 71)*.

OPEN STRINGER

NOSING

AN ALTERNATIVE FOR A SOLID BULLNOSE

INSERT

INSERT

1. Installing the insert.
◆ At the newel-post mark on the bullnose *(page 92, Step 1)*, drill a pilot hole for the insert slightly deeper than its length.
◆ Using the nut-and-bolt assembly provided with the insert *(photograph)*, screw it into the tread with an adjustable wrench *(left)*. Unscrew and discard the nuts and bolt to make way for the hanger bolt *(photograph, bottom)* that joins the newel post to the tread.

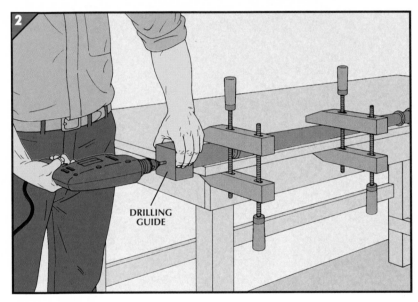

DRILLING GUIDE

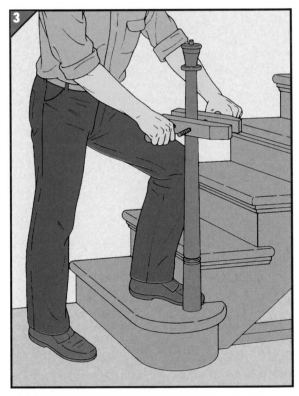

2. Drilling the starting newel.
◆ Cut the newel post to the height determined by your building code.
◆ Drill a plumb hole for the hanger bolt's wood-threaded end through scrap wood at least 2 inches thick to use as a drilling guide for a hanger-bolt pilot hole in the tread.
◆ Clamp the post to a workbench and center the guide on the bottom of the post. Drill a pilot hole $\frac{1}{2}$ inch deeper than the length of the bolt's wood-threaded end *(above)*.
◆ Screw the bolt into the post, gripping the unthreaded center section with locking pliers.

HANGER BOLT

3. Attaching the newel post.
◆ Screw the post into the insert in the bullnose tread. Tighten the post with a wooden hand-screw clamp padded with a dry rag to avoid marring the post *(above)*.
◆ Check the post for plumb with a 4-foot level. Sand the bottom of the post on one side if necessary to make it stand vertically.
◆ For the final fit, apply glue to the bottom of the post and tighten it in place.

FITTING A LANDING NEWEL

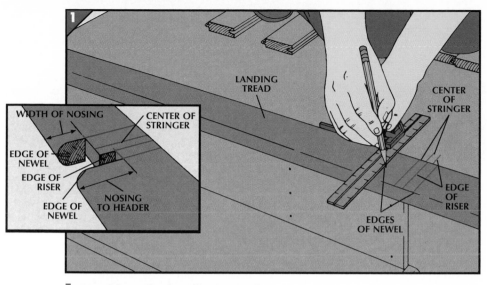

1. Notching the landing tread.
◆ With a combination square, mark the outer edge of the top riser and the center of the open stringer on the landing subfloor.
◆ Slide the end of the landing tread into the matching notch in the housed stringer, and transfer the marks on the landing subfloor to the tread.
◆ Measure the width of the landing newel, then mark on the tread where the newel's edges will fall when it is centered on the stringer mark.
◆ Measure the width of the tread nosing and the distance from the front of the nosing to the header; transfer both the measurements to the face of the tread *(inset)*, then shade the area that must be notched for the landing newel.
◆ Cut out the notch with a router or a saw and chisel, then drill pilot holes through the landing tread and fasten it to the subfloor and header with $2\frac{1}{2}$-inch finishing nails.

2. Adding the finish-floor line.
◆ On the landing newel post, choose and mark the front—the side to which the gooseneck will be attached—thereby also determining the back and the open side of the post *(page 65)*.
◆ On the front, mark a line where the top of the gooseneck will be, as specified by the building code.
◆ Add the length of the gooseneck's drop (provided by the manufacturer) and the rail height required by your building code. Starting at the gooseneck mark, measure this distance down the newel, and make a mark indicating the finish-floor line across the back and sides of the newel *(above)*.

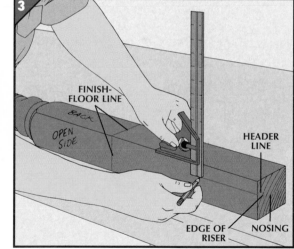

3. Notching the landing newel.
◆ On the newel bottom, measure from the front and mark the width of the landing-tread nosing *(Step 1, above)* and the distance from the nosing to the header.
◆ Measuring from the open side of the newel, mark the edge of the riser *(Step 1, above)*.
◆ Use a combination square to extend the nosing and header lines up the sides of the newel to the finish-floor line.
◆ With a router and rabbeting bit or a chisel and mallet, cut away the wood in the shaded area from the bottom of the newel to the finish-floor line.

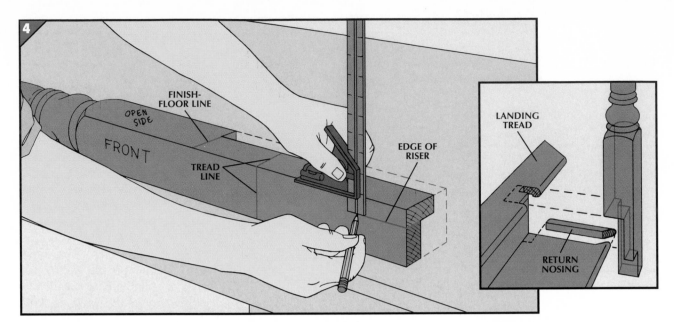

4. Fitting the newel to the stringer.

◆ On the stairway, measure the distance from the top of the landing tread to the tread below it and, measuring down the newel from the finish-floor line *(page 95, Step 2)*, mark a tread line at this distance on all sides of the newel.

◆ Extend the riser line up the newel's front to the tread line. Shade the area to be removed to allow the newel to fit over the stringer, then cut out the notch with a router or chisel and mallet.

◆ Set the newel in position on the tread below the landing, pushing it against the riser, and mark the return nosing flush with the newel's front.

◆ Along the line you have just drawn, cut the return nosing and the molding beneath it *(page 65)*, and remove the pieces so that the newel can lie against the stringer *(inset).*

◆ Set the post in place to check whether it fits properly. Smooth the cuts with a sharp chisel to bring the post snugly against the riser, stringer, and cutouts in the landing tread.

◆ Securely fasten the post to the header and stringer with countersunk wood screws and trim washers, and plug the holes.

ASSEMBLING THE RAILING

1. Cutting the gooseneck.

◆ Prepare a pitch block—a right-angle triangle of wood with sides equal to the unit rise and unit run of the stairs *(page 86)*—and have your helper hold a framing square upright with the block in its corner, run side down.

◆ Set the vertical part of the goose-neck tight against the framing square and mark the point where the pitch block touches the gooseneck *(right).*

◆ With the rise side of the pitch block on a workbench alongside the framing square, hold the gooseneck against the tongue and, using the block as a straightedge, extend the mark into a line across the railing *(far right).*

◆ Cut the gooseneck along this line in a power miter box.

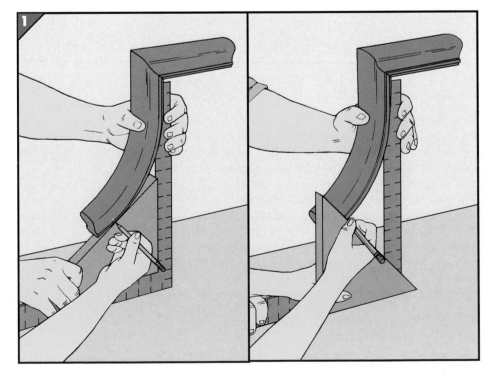

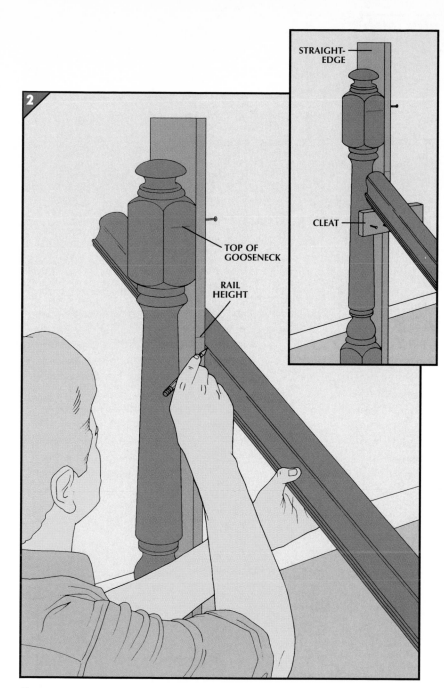

STRAIGHT-EDGE

TOP OF GOOSENECK

RAIL HEIGHT

CLEAT

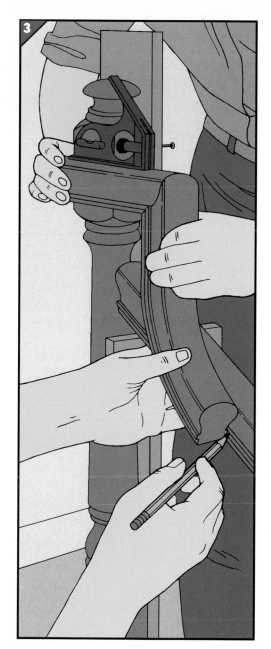

2. Bracing the rail in place.

◆ Temporarily nail a straight 1-inch board to the side of the landing newel, flush with the front of the newel.

◆ Measuring up from the landing tread, mark the board at the rail height.

◆ At the bottom of the stairs, tap the volute in place on the dowel of the starting newel with a rubber mallet while a helper supports the attached rail. Hold the upper end of the rail alongside the landing newel at the marked height and, using the temporary board as a guide, draw a line on the rail's edge *(above)*.

◆ Remove the volute and rail and cut the rail along this line with a power miter box.

◆ Reposition the volute on the newel and, with a combination square, align the top of the rail with the mark on the straightedge *(inset)*. Position the rail with a temporary cleat nailed or clamped to the board and newel.

3. Cutting the rail.

◆ Have a helper hold the gooseneck alongside the landing newel at the correct height above the finish floor *(page 95, Step 2)*, with about 6 inches of the horizontal section in front of the newel.

◆ Level the horizontal section with a combination square *(above)* or torpedo level, then mark where the bottom of the gooseneck intersects the rail.

◆ Remove the volute and rail and, with a power miter box, cut the rail square at the mark.

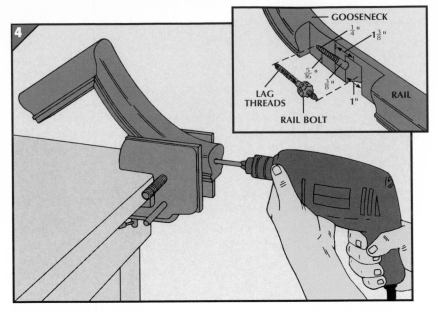

4. Installing the rail bolt.

◆ Clamp the gooseneck in a vise and, as shown above, drill a $\frac{1}{4}$-inch hole in the end, $\frac{15}{16}$ of an inch above the bottom of the gooseneck and $1\frac{7}{8}$ inches deep.

◆ Drill a matching $\frac{3}{8}$-inch hole in the end of the rail *(inset)*.

◆ Mark the center of the railing bottom, $1\frac{3}{8}$ inches from the rail end, and drill a hole at this point, 1 inch wide and $1\frac{1}{2}$ inches deep. Be careful not to drill through the railing.

◆ Screw the lag-threaded end of a rail bolt, ordered from the stair company, into the gooseneck. Run the nut onto the bolt as far as possible; turn the nut with an adjustable wrench to tighten the lag threads in the gooseneck.

◆ Remove the nut and washer and insert the free end of the bolt into the end of the rail. Run the washer and nut onto the bolt through the hole in the rail bottom and tighten the nut with a nail set and hammer.

5. Fitting gooseneck to newel.

◆ With the volute in place on the starting newel, hold the gooseneck alongside the landing newel as shown above, and mark the gooseneck where it meets the newel.

◆ Unbolt the rail and cut the gooseneck at this mark with a power miter box, then refasten the rail. Trim the gooseneck's end in $\frac{1}{8}$-inch increments until it fits snugly against the front of the newel.

◆ Fasten the gooseneck to the newel with a rail bolt using the method described in Step 4.

ADDING THE BALUSTERS

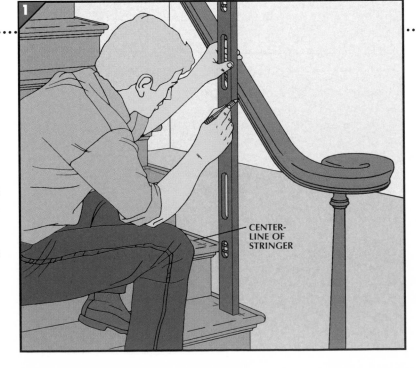

1. Positioning the balusters.

◆ Under the stair, measure from the wall to the center of the open stringer and draw a line the same distance from the wall on each tread, excluding the starting tread.

◆ Mark two baluster locations along this line, so the front of one is over the front of the riser below and the second is halfway between the back of the first and the front of the riser behind.

◆ Holding a 4-foot level plumb at each baluster location, make corresponding marks on the railing side *(right)*, then use a combination square to transfer the marks to the underside.

◆ Mark the underside of the volute with the paper template *(page 92, Step 1)*.

◆ Using spade bits matched to the balusters' dowels, drill holes $\frac{3}{4}$ inch deep into the treads, and 1 inch deep into the volute and railing.

Installing Wall-to-Wall Carpet

Carpet laying was once an art performed by skilled workers who stitched every seam and placed each hidden tack to carpet even a small room. Today's special tools and materials—tackless strip *(page 104)*, heat-sealing seaming tape *(page 110)*, and the knee-kicker and power stretcher *(pages 111 and 112)*—have so simplified laying carpet that even an amateur can do it.

Styles of Piles: Most carpets are tufted: that is, their pile—the fibers that make up the cushiony surface—is machine stitched into a backing. Carpets may be made with loop pile or cut pile *(bottom left)*, a distinction that is important when cutting carpet *(page 107)*.

When new carpet is rolled up as it comes off the machine, the pile fibers are pressed down, acquiring a "pile direction" that permanently affects appearance and installation technique *(checklist, right)*.

Measuring the Room: The first step in a carpeting project is to determine how much carpet you will need to buy. Begin by drawing the room to scale on graph paper, letting each square equal 1 square foot. Measure the length of each wall and the distances between doorjambs and other features, and plot the measurements on the graph paper. Also measure between the walls in several places to see if they are skewed or bowed. Add 4 inches to the length and the width of the floor to allow for error and for trimming each factory-cut edge.

Estimating Carpet Needs: Cut a strip of graph paper 12 squares wide to represent the standard 12-foot width of broadloom carpet. Snip pieces from the strip and arrange them on your room diagram to keep wasted carpet to a minimum. Consult the checklist and the illustrations at right for tips on how to place seams and position the pile.

With patterned carpet, you must take into account the repeat—the distance from the point where a pattern begins to where it begins again—in order to be sure of matching the pattern along a seam.

Padding and Tackless Strip: Your scale drawing will also tell you how much padding and tackless strip you need. Padding comes in rolls $4\frac{1}{2}$ to 12 feet wide; compute the square footage of the room and buy just a little more than will cover the area. Determine the type of tackless strip needed *(page 104)*, and buy a few feet more than the room's perimeter. (If you are replacing a carpet with one that is of similar thickness, use the existing strip. Make sure the strip pins are at the proper angle and that the strip is nailed down securely.)

Before starting, reattach loose flooring, remove grilles from heating vents, and sweep the floor. You might wish to remove shoe moldings; if you do not plan to reinstall them, repaint the baseboards before laying the carpet.

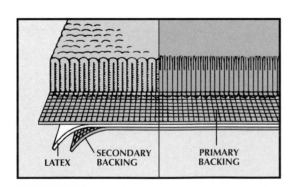

| LATEX | SECONDARY BACKING | PRIMARY BACKING |

Tufted carpet.

The pile yarn of tufted carpet is stitched through a layer of open-weave fabric—the primary backing. A second fabric backing is stuck onto the underside of the first with a coating of latex. When the yarn is left uncut, the result is loop-pile carpet *(left)*. But the tops of the loops are often split or cut off, making cut-pile carpet *(right)*.

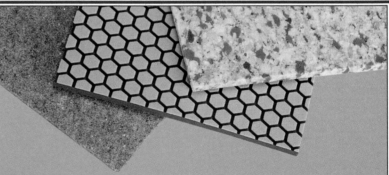

CHOOSING A CARPET PAD

Most carpet padding is made either of synthetic felt, a mix of foam and rubber scraps bonded together in sheets, or a continuous sheet of urethane foam. Felt, a hard padding, is now rarely used in homes, having been supplanted by the other two. Bonded and urethane padding come in a variety of densities and thicknesses. Urethane is the more expensive of the two, but either in higher grades will outlast most carpets.

Buy a pad $\frac{7}{16}$ inch thick or less; thicker pads flex too much, causing damage to the carpet backing. Medium- or high-density pads extend the life of a carpet.

FITTING CARPET TO THE ROOM

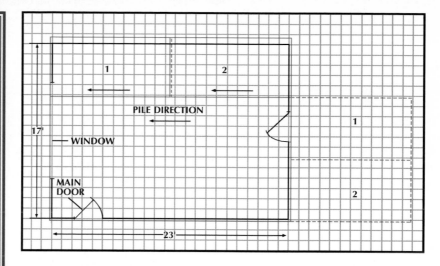

Carpet Layer's Checklist

✔ Keep seams away from high-traffic areas, such as doorways, where they could become loose.

✔ Run the room's longest seam toward the major light source—usually the largest window. A seam running parallel to light rays is much less apparent than one running across them.

✔ Stroke the carpet to find its pile direction: stroking against the pile direction raises the nap. Install carpet with the pile leaning toward the main entrance, to present its richest appearance.

✔ Within a room the pile of every section of carpet must lean the same way, or the pieces will show up as different hues.

Lengthwise installation.

In this typical room, 17 feet by 23 feet, the best plan is lengthwise installation of broadloom 12 feet wide; the rest is filled with two pieces *(1 and 2)* from an extra 4 yards of carpet *(dashed lines, far right)*. The major seam will run into the main light source—the window at the left. The pile should lean toward the main door. Most of the room's traffic will pass between the two doors, over the large section of full-width carpet. The seams will be out of the way, and probably partly hidden by furniture.

In a smaller room, fill the gap between the main run of carpet and the wall at the top of the drawing with narrow sections cut from the 12-foot broadloom width. You will have to make more seams but pay for less carpet.

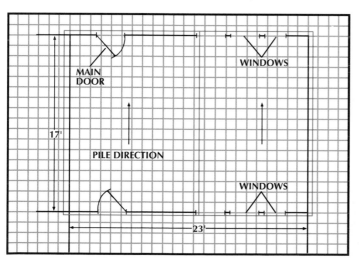

Short sheeting a room.

This room *(left),* while the same size as that above, has an arrangement of doors and windows that makes it preferable to install the length of the carpet across the shorter dimension of the room—a technique that is called short sheeting. That way, the major seam will be aligned with the light from the windows and will be away from the bulk of traffic that passes between the doors. The pile should lean toward the main door.

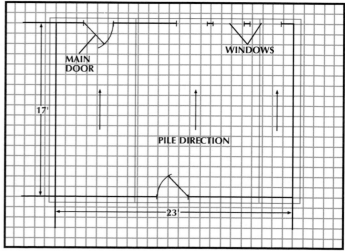

Adding a seam to avoid a door.

This room is much like that above, center, except that a door is in the middle of one wall and the seam of a normal short-sheeting installation would run directly into it, taking the wear of heavy traffic. To avoid this undesirable seam location, cut one of the full widths of carpet lengthwise into two pieces and seam them to both sides of the remaining full-width section. The result is two seams instead of one, but neither of them runs directly into a door.

A Foundation of Padding and Pins

Although hidden when the job is done, tackless strip and padding are essential to the carpeting of a room. The tackless strip goes around the perimeter of the room to hold the carpet taut *(below);* the padding provides cushioning.

Get the Correct Strip: Tackless strip comes in three main types, all 1 inch wide and $\frac{1}{4}$ inch thick, with two rows of pins. Type C strip, with pins $\frac{1}{4}$ inch high, is used for thick shag carpeting. Type D strip has $\frac{3}{16}$-inch pins suited for thin-backed carpets. Type E has medium-sized $\frac{7}{32}$-inch pins that are right for the great majority of carpets.

To select the right type of strip, place a sample of carpet over the pins and press your fingers into the carpet. The carpet and strip are ideally matched if you can discern the tips of the pins without being pricked by them. If the pins feel sharp, use strip with shorter pins.

A fourth type, called architectural strip, is $1\frac{1}{2}$ inches wide and has three rows of pins to grasp carpet more firmly. This strip is better for laying heavy-backed or woven carpets, and for installing carpet in very large rooms.

Installing the Strip: The tackless strip is nailed to most floors but can be glued to tiles. You can nail it through vinyl tiles, but if a concrete floor lies under the tile, use strip that has masonry nails.

Place strip in front of obstacles such as radiators, under which it would be difficult to stretch the carpet. Where carpet will end in a doorway, use special metal edging *(opposite, bottom).*

Laying Carpet Padding: Always put padding down smooth or shiny side up. With wood sub- or finish flooring, all forms of padding are stapled in place after being cut *(page 106).* However, other circumstances require different measures.

On concrete or ceramic tile, use linoleum paste to cement down felt padding. Affix foam-rubber padding to concrete or tile using an adhesive made for that purpose. Secure the seams between sections with padding tape, and tape the pad to the strip by pushing the tape over the pins across the strip's full width.

 TOOLS

Hammer	Staple gun
Saw	Utility knife
Garden shears	

 **MATERIALS**

Tackless strip	Sandpaper
Cardboard	Water-based
Metal edging	adhesive

 SAFETY TIPS

Wear goggles when hammering nails and when cutting tackless strip. Gloves protect your hands when you are working with tackless strip.

Holding carpet without tacks.

Tackless strip is made of a three-ply strip of wood 1 inch wide and $\frac{9}{32}$ inch thick, with sharp pins protruding at a 60-degree angle from the face to grip the carpet. When the strip is installed correctly, the pins point toward the wall, and the printing on the strip can be read from the room. It comes in 4-foot lengths and is fixed to the floor with preset nails. Strip with masonry nails for concrete floors is available.

When carpet is stretched over the strip, the pins hold it under tension. A gully formed between the wall and the strip holds the tucked-in edge of the carpet. The strip comes beveled along the wall edge to create a gully if you leave quarter-round shoe moldings in place.

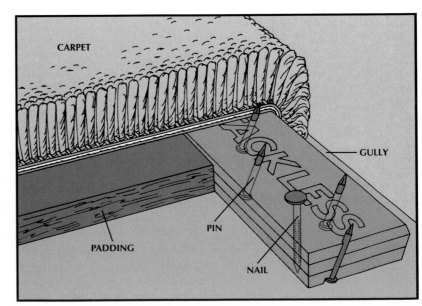

CARPET

GULLY

PADDING

PIN

NAIL

NAILING TACKLESS STRIP TO THE FLOOR

1. Fastening strips along a wall.
◆ Glue pieces of cardboard together to make a spacer two-thirds the thickness of the carpet.
◆ Starting in a corner, use the spacer to position a length of tackless strip next to the wall, and drive the nails into the floor.

If you cannot keep from battering down the carpet-holding pins with a regular hammer, try a tack hammer, which has a smaller head. When nailing into concrete, you will need a ball-peen hammer with a 24-ounce head.

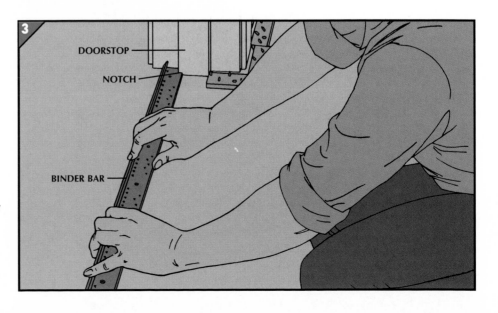

2. Cutting tackless strip.
With a saw or garden shears, cut pieces to fit around a doorjamb *(left)*, or to fill gaps. If using shears, grip the strip in the jaws, position the lower handle against the floor, and lean on the upper handle to make the cut. At door openings install small pieces to maintain the correct spacing between the strip and each section of door molding. Drive extra nails so that each piece of strip is held by at least two.

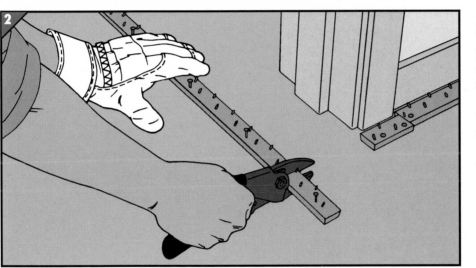

3. Metal edging for doorways.
Nail metal edging to the floor so that its binder bar—the flange that folds down over the carpet edge—is directly under the door. In doorways where the door opens away from the area to be carpeted, as shown at right, notch the flat part of the strip to accommodate the doorstop.

FASTENING TACKLESS STRIP WITH GLUE

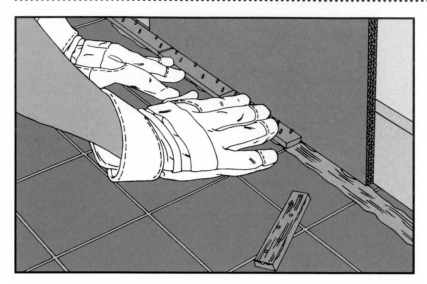

Cementing strip.
◆ On an uneven, nonnailable surface such as a ceramic tile floor, cut the strip to the width of each tile—if the tiles are very small, cut the strips about 4 inches long.
◆ Clean and sand the floor surface, then fasten each strip with a water-based adhesive, tapping each piece with a tack hammer in order to make a strong joint.

LAYING THE PAD

1. Stapling padding in place.
◆ Cut from the roll of padding a piece large enough to cover one end of the room, slightly overlapping the tackless strip.
◆ Drive staples at 6-inch intervals around the edges of the piece.
◆ Cut and staple down more padding, butting the pieces together, until the floor is covered.

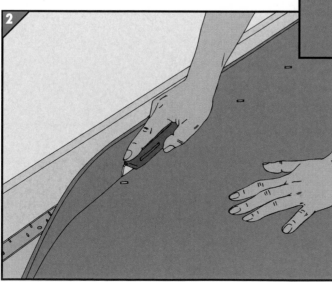

2. Trimming.
With a utility knife make a vertical cut along the inside edge of the tackless strip all around the room. For foam padding that is thicker than the tackless strip, tilt the knife away from the wall to make a beveled edge. Doing so will ensure that the padding will not ride up over the strip when you stretch the carpet over it.

Unroll the carpet and cut it according to the graph-paper plan you made earlier *(page 103)*, then stack the pieces and give them time to flatten.

Lay out the pieces in the area to be carpeted so that the pile leans in the same direction on all of them.

Cutting Techniques: Cutting on the pile side of the carpet, called front-cutting, is used on loop-pile carpet *(page 102)* to be sure the carpet does not remain joined by uncut loops across the cut. Front-cutting is also preferred for cut-pile carpet if you can find the space between rows of pile. Cutting carpet across its backing—back-cutting—is reserved for cut-pile with indistinct rows of pile.

Seams across the width of the carpet require special care to ensure a perfect fit *(page 109)*.

In a doorway, make the seam only after the carpet on one side has been stretched and fastened to metal edging *(page 114)*.

Carpet Tools: Front-cutting is easier when you use a row-running cutter *(below)*. This inexpensive tool has a runner that slips between rows of pile while a sharp blade behind the runner cuts the carpet backing without harming the pile.

A utility knife suffices for other cutting jobs, but a carpet knife, available where you buy carpet, has a two-edged, flexible blade that makes some cutting tasks easier.

Seams are sealed with hot-melt seaming tape and a seaming iron *(page 110)*, available for rent. The tape glues seams tightly together from the underside.

 TOOLS

Row-running cutter
Straightedge
Chalk line
Utility knife or carpet knife
Seaming iron

 **MATERIALS**

Hot-melt seaming tape (6" wide)
Edge sealer

TWO WAYS TO CUT CARPET

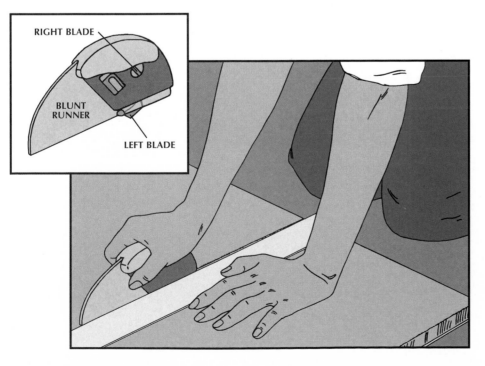

RIGHT BLADE

BLUNT RUNNER

LEFT BLADE

Front-cutting.
◆ Measure and mark the carpet.
◆ Retract both blades of a row-running cutter *(inset)*. Place the runner between two rows of pile, and slide the runner across the carpet.
◆ After making a path through the pile, extend the blade on the side of the tool next to the section of carpet you will use and make the cut, guided by a straightedge.

Back-cutting.

◆ Measure along the face of the un-rolled carpet, cut notches in the edges to mark the cutting location, then fold the carpet back.

◆ Stretch a chalk line taut between the notches, then snap the line.

◆ Extend the blade of a carpet knife enough to cut the backing only, and slice along the chalked line guided by a straightedge.

MANEUVERING THE CARPET

1. Kicking carpet into place.

◆ Lay a cut piece of carpet on the section of floor it will cover. Lift a corner, straddle it, and kick the carpet to shift it into its final position *(right)*. Kick with your toe or the side of your foot; using your heel may tear the carpet.

◆ At both inside corners and outside corners, slit the carpet vertically where it laps up against the baseboard *(inset)*. Cut only as far as the bottom of the baseboard. Doing so allows the carpet on both sides of the corner to lie flat on the floor.

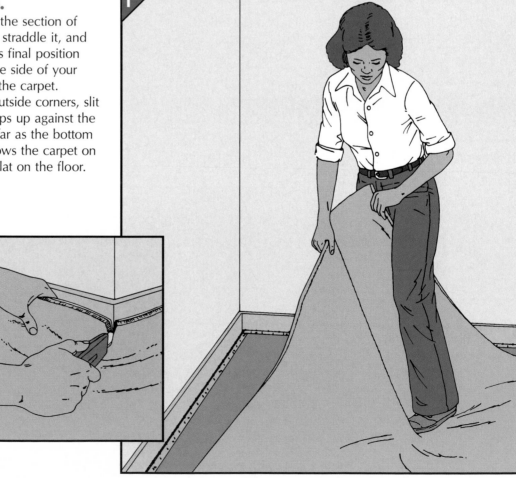

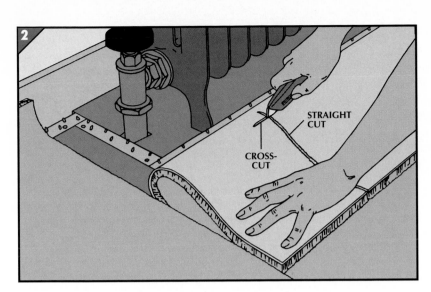

2. Cutting to fit around obstacles.

◆ Fold the carpet so that the backing touches an obstacle, such as the foot of a radiator, and mark the backing there. Make a straight cut from the mark to the carpet's edge.

◆ Then make a crosscut just long enough for the carpet to lie roughly flat around the obstacle until final trimming. For a radiator this may involve several cuts out to the edge and several crosscuts to accommodate all the feet and pipes.

MAKING A HOT-MELT SEAM

1. Cutting for a cross seam.

◆ Where you need to make a seam across the width of the carpet roll, overlap the pieces 1 inch, placing on top the piece that has its pile leaning toward the joint. Make sure the edge of this piece is positioned between pile rows on the piece below and parallel to them.

◆ With the edge of the top piece as a guide, cut the underlying carpet with a row-running cutter *(inset).*

◆ Cut the part of the carpet that laps the wall with a utility knife.

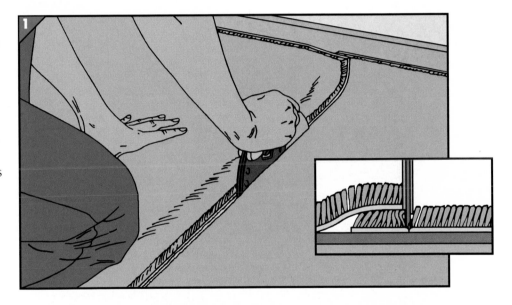

Wavy Seams for Sculptured Carpet

TRICKS OF THE TRADE

Because sculptured carpet's multilevel surface and swirl design are difficult to match at a seam, straight seams are unpleasantly obvious. A serpentine tool allows you to cut a wavy edge for a less apparent seam.

When cutting the two adjoining pieces, offset the tool the width of one "hump" from one piece to the next so that the convex cutouts on one side of the seam fit into the concave portions on the butting piece.

The opposite edge of the tool serves as a long straightedge for other types of cuts.

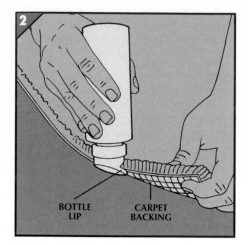

BOTTLE
LIP

CARPET
BACKING

2. Sealing the cut edge.

Edge sealer coats carpet backing along a cut with a fast-drying liquid, preventing the edges from fraying. Practice with the sealer on a piece of scrap carpet so that you can apply it evenly and without getting the liquid on the pile. Apply sealer as follows:

◆ Push the activator button on the sealer bottle, then invert the container.

◆ Place the lip of the bottle against the backing. Squeeze the bottle lightly as you move it at a smooth and consistent speed along the carpet edge.

◆ Seal all cut edges of carpet.

3. Positioning seaming tape.

Slip a length of hot-melt seaming tape, adhesive side up, under one edge of carpet where two pieces will be joined. Align the tape's printed centerline with the carpet edge.

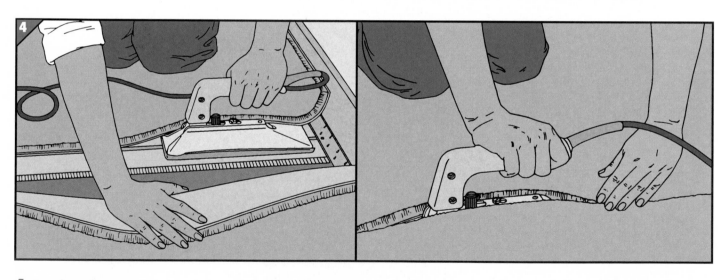

4. Ironing the tape.

◆ Warm a seaming iron to 250°—setting number two on some models.

◆ Holding back the carpet on one side of the joint, slip the preheated iron onto the tape at the end that lets you work along the direction of the pile *(above, left)*. Center the iron on the tape; allow the carpet to flop down.

◆ Let the iron rest for 30 seconds. Then draw it slowly along the tape for a distance of about 1 foot while you press the carpet into the softened adhesive behind the iron *(above, right)*.

◆ Separate the pile along the seam to check that the carpet backings touch; if not, force them together with your hands, then weight the seam with a board at least 6 inches by 2 feet.

◆ Continue seaming about a foot at a time, moving the board along the seam and kneeling on it as you go. Work as close as you can to the wall, then wait 5 minutes for the adhesive to set.

◆ To finish the final few inches of seam at the carpet edge, slide the carpet away from the wall to free the iron.

> *Do not use a household iron on seaming tape. A seaming iron has a heat shield to direct heat against the tape and away from the carpet's underside.*
>
> **CAUTION**

After you have rough-cut and seamed a carpet, you will need two tools, available at rental agencies, to make it smooth and taut. The first, a knee-kicker, secures an edge of the carpet to the tackless strip and to metal edging across doorways along one wall. The second is called a power stretcher. Used in concert with a knee-kicker, it pulls the carpet across the room and secures it to the strip along the opposite wall.

Hooking the Carpet on the Pins: The knee-kicker has an adjustable gripping head on one end, a cushion on the other, and an adjustable telescoping handle in between. Forced into the pile at one edge of your carpet, tiny hooks in the gripping head catch the nap and longer teeth extend through the carpet backing. When you bump the kicking cushion, or pad, with your knee, the knee-kicker scoots forward, carrying the carpet toward the wall; if you have placed the tool correctly, the carpet will remain against the wall, caught by the pins in the tackless strip.

Stretching It Tight: After securing the carpet at one wall, stretch it across the room with a power stretcher. Like a knee-kicker, a power stretcher has a toothed head, but it is a larger device—as much as 26 feet long when fully extended. A smaller version, called a ministretcher, is intended for narrow places such as hallways.

Instead of jerking the carpet into position like a knee-kicker, stretchers have a smoothly operating lever action that pulls the carpet and locks the toothed head in place to hold the carpet at the correct tension. A 2-by-4 and a 2-by-8 come in handy when using a power stretcher opposite a doorway and in very large rooms *(page 112)*.

Trimming and Tucking: After attaching the carpet to the tackless strip all the way around the room, trim the excess and tuck the edge into the gully between the baseboard and the strip. This hides the cut edges of the carpet and locks it securely to the strip.

You can do the trimming with a utility knife, but a special tool called a wall trimmer—which can be rented—does the job more precisely. Finally, trim the carpet around floor duct openings (making sure that grilles cover raw carpet edges) and plane doors so they clear the carpet.

TOOLS

Knee-kicker	Power stretcher
Ministretcher	Wall trimmer
	Screwdriver
	Hammer

USING A KNEE-KICKER

Hooking the first edge of the carpet.
◆ Before using the kicker, adjust its head until you can feel the teeth on the underside of a scrap of carpet.
◆ Place the head of the kicker in the carpet no more than 4 inches from the wall. Then push the extension release trigger to adjust the handle to a comfortable length.
◆ Lean on the handle with one hand, and bring your knee smartly against the kicking cushion *(right)*. The carpet, shoved forward, should catch on the tackless strip, and the excess will lap farther up the wall.
◆ As you move along the wall, hold the already secured carpet in place with your free hand so that it does not come unhooked as you kick.

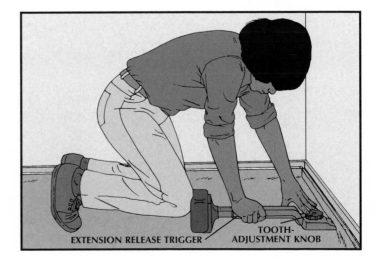

EXTENSION RELEASE TRIGGER
TOOTH-ADJUSTMENT KNOB

Knee-kicking in narrow places.
In restricted spaces like hallways, strike the pad with the side of your knee *(far left)* or adjust the handle so that you can place your foot against the wall and your knee against the kicker pad *(near left);* then force the kicker to move by pushing against the wall with your foot.

POWER STRETCHER TECHNIQUES

Stretching a carpet.
◆ Set the stretcher's teeth for your carpet thickness, and adjust its extension tubes so that it reaches from the wall where you used the knee-kicker to a point 6 inches from the opposite wall. In narrow places, use a ministretcher *(photograph).*
◆ Press the lever down gently to avoid tearing the carpet. If the lever locks before the carpet is fully stretched, release the tension and extend the stretcher one notch. When the lever will not lock without overstretching the carpet, reset the head with the lever partly lowered.
◆ Use the face of a hammer to press the carpet firmly onto the pins in the tackless strip.

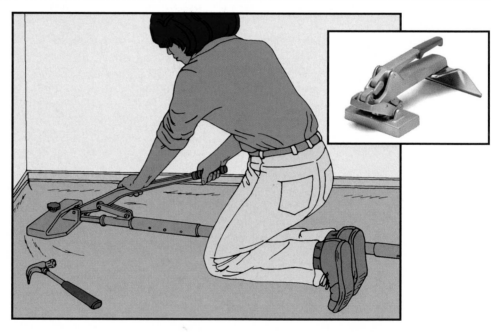

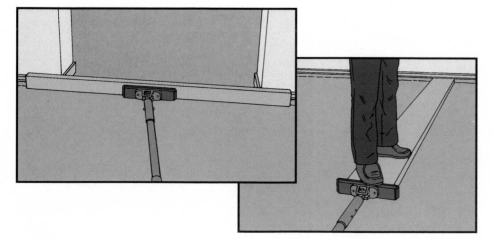

Ways to brace the stretcher.
◆ If there is a doorway in the wall you are stretching from, bridge it with a 2-by-4 *(far left),* which will serve as a brace for the tail block.
◆ If your room is longer than the maximum length of the stretcher—usually 26 feet—use a 2-by-8 between the tail block and the wall to extend the reach of the device *(near left).* Have a helper stand on the board so that it will not slip out of place during the stretch.

WHEN AND WHERE TO KICK AND STRETCH

Fitting a taut carpet.

These pictures show the sequence in which to use a knee-kicker and a power stretcher to lay a carpet in a typical room.

◆ Begin by hooking the carpet in one corner *(1)* with a knee-kicker and stretch it to an opposite wall with the power stretcher at a slight angle.

◆ Then secure the carpet against the perpendicular wall near the same corner *(2)* with a knee-kicker and stretch it to the opposite wall with the power stretcher.

◆ Next, hook the carpet with the knee-kicker the full length of the top and right-hand walls *(3 and 4)* at about a 15-degree angle, then use the power stretcher along the bottom wall *(5)* at a similar angle.

◆ Finally, stretch from the right-hand wall to the left-hand wall *(6)*.

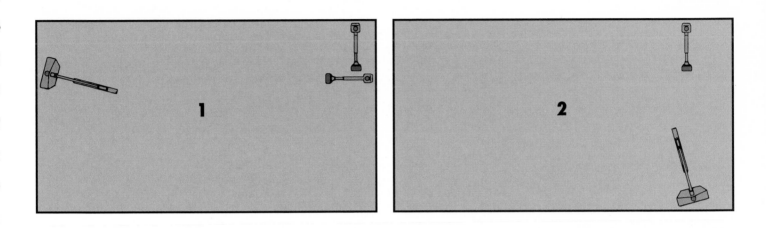

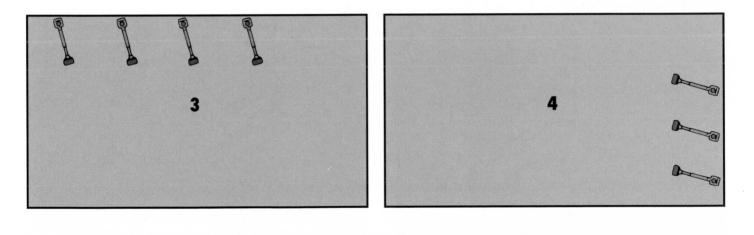

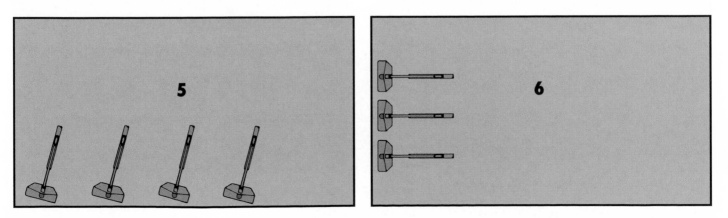

THE FINAL TRIM AND FIT

1. Trimming the carpet.

◆ Adjust a wall trimmer for the thickness of carpet and trim the edges of the carpet all around the room. Start the trimmer in the up-lapping carpet at a 45-degree angle and level it out when you reach the floor.

◆ Trim the last few inches approaching a wall with a utility knife.

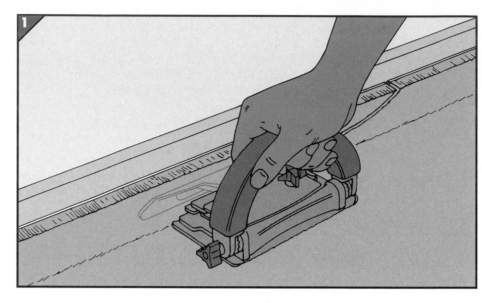

2. Tucking in the carpet.

Put masking tape on the tip of a screwdriver, and use it to tuck the carpet into the gully between the tackless strip and the baseboard and to snare any loose strands of yarn in the gully. If the carpet edge bulges after tucking, pull it out of the gully and trim it a bit shorter before retucking.

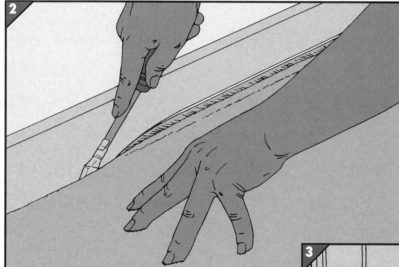

3. Clamping the carpet at a metal edge.

◆ Trim the carpet to fit under the binder bar of a metal edging strip.

◆ Tuck the carpet under the binder bar and bend it against the carpet by gently tapping a block of wood with a hammer *(right)*. Bend the bar down a little at a time by moving the block of wood along it after each hammer blow to avoid deforming the edging.

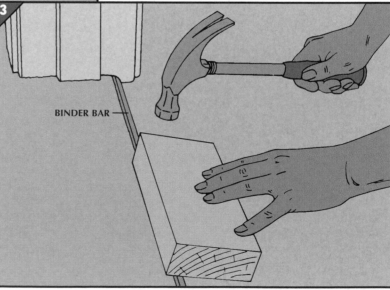

BINDER BAR

Stairs deserve high-quality carpeting. The nap of a cheap carpet with a low pile density will soon wear away there, exposing the carpet backing in an effect called "grinning."

Help preserve your carpet by using a high-density padding beneath it *(page 102)*. Another way to increase carpet life, by up to half, is to let the pile of the carpet lean toward the nosing.

How Much Carpet to Buy: When estimating the amount of carpet needed, first measure the width of a stair baluster-to-baluster, baluster-to-wall, or wall-to-wall. Add $2\frac{1}{2}$ inches to allow for a $1\frac{1}{4}$-inch roll-under on each side *(page 118, Step 4)*, then deduct twice the height of the pile. Doing so assures that the pile will just brush walls and balusters when the carpet is installed. If the result is 36 inches or less, you can get four stair-width pieces from a standard 12-foot-wide roll of broadloom.

To estimate the number of running yards of broadloom to buy for a straight flight of stairs, first divide the number of steps by the number of stair-width pieces you can obtain from a standard roll of carpeting. Next multiply the result by the amount of carpeting needed to cover one step *(below)*, and add a foot or so as a safety margin. After buying a piece of carpet this length, cut it into strips as shown on pages 107 and 108.

Dealing with Corners: When a stairway turns a corner, find the amount of carpet you will need for its wedge-shaped steps by cutting paper templates. Make a separate template for each tread and the riser below, adding 1 inch to allow for the bulge of padding over tread nosings. Cut the templates to a width that takes into consideration pile height and a $1\frac{1}{4}$-inch roll-under next to balusters, but not next to walls.

Cover each template with a piece of carpet, then grasp both carpet and template and turn them over. Align the template's bottom edge between two rows of pile and cut around the template.

Attach the carpet cutout to the tackless strip on the riser and stretch it over the tread. If the wall has a pronounced curve on its closed side, cut the tackless strip into small pieces that follow the arc. On an open side, roll the carpet edge under and tack it into place.

The Runner Option: A runner can be tufted carpet or an Oriental rug. Both work best on a straight stairway; leave a curved one to professionals. Measure as shown below, but do not cut an Oriental runner to fit; it will unravel. Instead, fold under any excess at the top, then tack it to the last riser. Add a decorative touch by affixing stair rods at the crotch of each step *(page 119)*.

 TOOLS

Tape measure
Hammer
Utility knife
Staple gun

Chalk line
Awl
Knee-kicker
Stair tool
1 x 3 gauge
  block

Electric drill with
  bits ($\frac{3}{32}$", $\frac{1}{8}$")
Handsaw
Screwdriver

 **MATERIALS**

Carpet
Tackless strip
Carpet tacks
  (24-ounce)

 **SAFETY TIPS**

Wear goggles when hammering nails and when cutting tackless strip. Gloves protect your hands when you are working with tackless strip.

PREPARING THE STAIRS

1. Determining the stairway length.

◆ Measure from the back of one tread to the bottom of the riser below *(right)* and add 1 inch for the bulge of padding at the tread nosing.
◆ Multiply this figure by the number of steps to be carpeted.

If you intend to carpet the landing at the top of the stairs, subtract the height of one riser.

In an old house the steps may be of varied sizes; in this situation measure each step individually and add the measurements together.

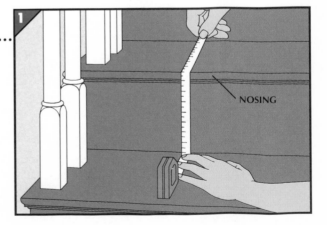

NOSING

2. Installing tackless strip.

◆ For each step, cut two pieces of tackless strip *(page 105, Step 2)* $2\frac{1}{2}$ inches shorter than the width of the steps.

◆ Make two spacers by pulling the nails from short pieces of tackless strip and taping them together, pins to pins *(inset)*.

◆ Rest a piece of tackless strip on the spacers and nail it to the riser, with the pins pointing down *(right)*. Nail tackless strip to the tread, $\frac{5}{8}$ inch from the riser and with the pins pointing toward it.

◆ Repeat the process for each riser and tread.

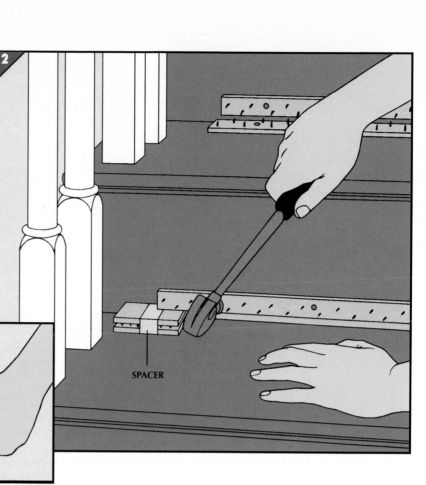

SPACER

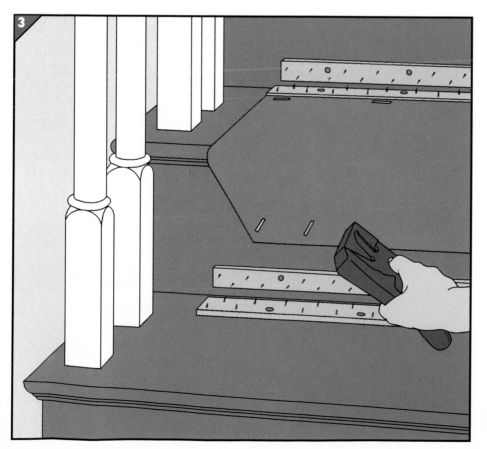

3. Fitting the padding.

◆ Cut a piece of padding $2\frac{1}{2}$ inches shorter than the width of a step. If one side of the stairway is open, cut the riser portion of the padding away from the nosing at an angle on the open side so that it will not be seen when carpeting is installed.

◆ Butt the padding against the tackless strip on a tread and staple it there.

◆ Pull the padding over the nose of the tread and staple it about 2 or 3 inches down the riser *(left)*.

LAYING THE CARPET

1. Rolling the edges.
◆ Lay the carpet facedown and snap a chalk line $1\frac{1}{4}$ inches from each side to mark the crease of the roll-under.
◆ Score the carpet backing along the chalked lines with an awl, folding the carpet with your fingers as you do so *(right)*.
◆ Position the carpet roughly on the stairway, with the pile leaning down the stairs.

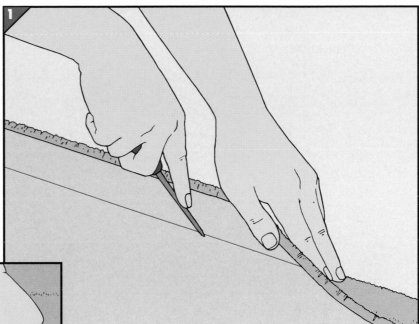

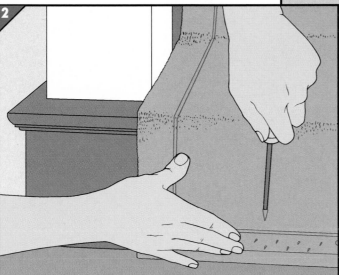

2. Securing the bottom edge.
◆ With an awl, pull the lower edge of the carpet over the tackless strip on the bottom riser until about $\frac{3}{8}$ inch laps onto the floor, then press the carpet onto the pins with your fingers *(left)*.
◆ Tuck the carpet edge into the gully between the tackless strip and floor. Run the head of a hammer along the gully to iron any bulges out of the carpet.
◆ Secure the rolled-under edge on each side with a 24-ounce carpet tack driven through both thicknesses of carpet and into the riser, just above the tackless strip.

3. Covering the tread.
◆ Beginning at the center of the bottom tread, stretch the carpet toward the stair riser with a knee-kicker. At the same time, push it into the gully behind the tackless strip with a stair tool, hooking the carpet backing on the pins of the strip *(right)*.
◆ Angle the knee-kicker slightly to stretch the carpet away from the center of the step, alternating left and right sides until you have done the entire step.

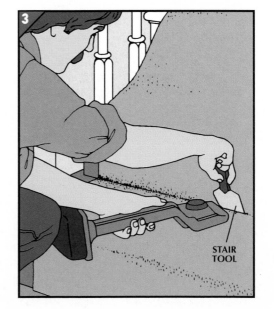

STAIR TOOL

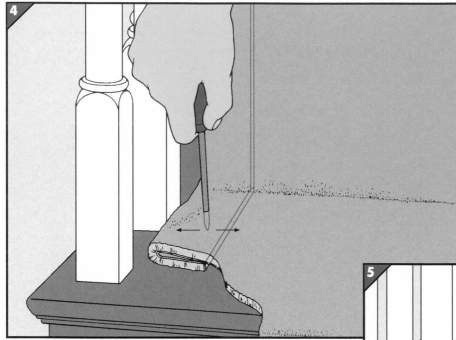

4. Adjusting the width.

If the width of a tread varies from front to back, push an awl through the top layer of the carpet's rolled-under edge, pierce the lower layer with the tip, and, using the awl as a lever, shift the rolled-under edge to make the carpet fit the width at every point.

5. Forcing the carpet into the crotch.

When you have adjusted the carpet the way you want it—trying to move it after this step will damage the backing—hammer the stair tool into the space between the tackless strips on the tread and riser *(right)*. Doing so tightens the carpet and fixes it securely to the tackless strip on the riser.

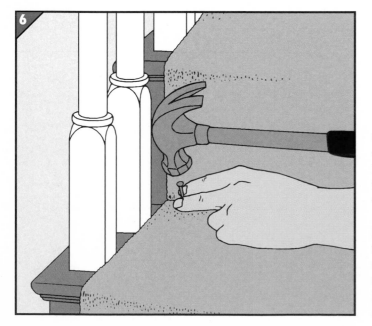

6. Tacking at the crotch.

◆ Secure the rolled edges at the tread-riser crotch with 24-ounce carpet tacks driven through the carpet and into the crotch at a point $\frac{5}{8}$ inch or less from each edge.
◆ Finish driving the tacks with a nail set if necessary.

Proceed up the stairs, one step at a time. When you reach the end of a length of carpet, drive a tack through each rolled-under edge near the rear of the tread, and trim off any carpet that extends beyond the tackless strip there. Begin fitting the next piece at the bottom of the next riser *(Step 2)*.

STAIR RODS FOR A RUNNER

1. Drilling rod-bracket holes.

To align the stair-rod brackets, make a gauge block for drilling the holes:

◆ Cut a piece of 1-by-3 equal in length to the width of a riser.

◆ Measure from the edges of the riser to the spot where the bracket will go—between $1\frac{1}{2}$ inches and 3 inches from balusters and walls and about $\frac{3}{4}$ inch above the tread.

◆ Transfer the measurements to the 1-by-3 and drill a $\frac{1}{8}$-inch hole through the board at each bracket location.

◆ Holding the block firmly in position against the riser, use the holes to guide a $\frac{3}{32}$-inch bit into the riser *(right)*.

◆ Drill holes on both sides of the step with the gauge block. For brackets that also screw into the tread, use the gauge block to drill holes there.

GAUGE BLOCK

STAIR ROD

RUNNER

2. Installing the runner.

◆ Screw the brackets onto each step, nail tackless strip between the brackets, and staple padding over the stair noses *(page 116, Steps 2 and 3)*.

◆ Starting at the bottom of the stairs and working one step at a time, install the runner as shown in Steps 2, 3, and 5 on pages 117 and 118.

◆ After securing the runner to a step, slide a stair rod into the corresponding brackets *(left)*. Screw one of the decorative caps provided onto each end of the rod.

◆ At the top of the staircase, tack the runner to the last riser, just below the nose of the landing.

The most carefully tended carpets can suffer accidental damage such as burns, rips, and stains. But with a few scraps of matching carpet and some inexpensive tools and materials, you can make durable, almost invisible repairs.

Set scraps aside when the carpet is laid or ask for some from the seller when you buy a carpeted house. If no scraps have been saved, take them from unseen areas such as a closet floor.

Carpet Repair Basics: Many repair jobs call for a tuft-setter, a special tool for embedding bits of pile yarn in the carpet backing. If you cannot find one at a carpet supplier, you can make your own *(opposite)*.

Before you begin to repair a damaged carpet, familiarize yourself with its special characteristics. Loop pile, for example, may require a different cutting technique *(page 107)* from the one that is used for cut pile, and the repairs for carpeting installed over padding are different from those for cushion-back carpeting *(page 125)*.

Always use the smallest piece of scrap carpet first, so that if you make a mistake there will be larger scraps available to correct it. Practice on carpet scraps before tackling the actual repair.

Cushion-Back Considerations: This type of carpet is glued to the floor instead of being stretched over tackless strips *(page 105)*, so some techniques cannot be used. For example, cushion-back carpet has only a single layer of woven backing

(conventional carpet has two), so mending a surface tear, as shown on page 124, will not work; the tear must be repaired by patching.

Cushion-back carpet is different in another way, as well: Although pile rows run straight along its length, as on a conventional carpet, the rows of pile running across the width of the roll sometimes meet the long rows diagonally.

Before cutting a patch, run the tip of a Phillips screwdriver along the crosswise rows at various angles until you can easily clear pathways for a utility knife. The resulting shape may be a parallelogram instead of a rectangle. Cut out the damaged area to fit the patch as you would on conventional carpet *(page 122)*, slicing through the cushion back all the way to the floor.

 TOOLS

Nail scissors
Tweezers
Cotton swabs
Tuft-setter
Hammer
Utility knife
Knee-kicker
Awl
Putty knife
Notched trowel ($\frac{3}{32}$")

 **MATERIALS**

Scrap carpet
Latex cement
Nails (1$\frac{1}{2}$")
Seam tape
Latex seam adhesive
Multipurpose flooring adhesive
Cushion-back seam adhesive

 **SAFETY TIPS**

Rubber gloves protect your hands when you are working with liquid adhesives.

RESTORING A SMALL AREA

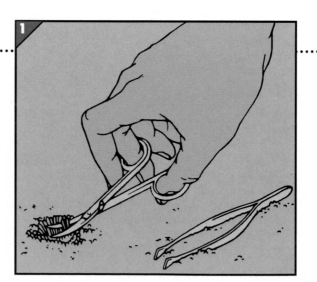

1. Removing damaged pile.
Using nail scissors *(right),* cut the damaged pile down to the carpet backing, then pick out the stubs of the tufts or loops with tweezers. For replacement pile, pick tufts or unravel lengths of looped yarn from the edge of a carpet scrap.

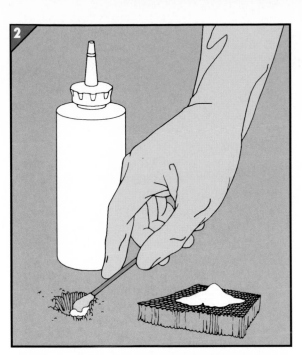

2. Applying the cement.

Squeeze a small amount of latex cement onto the back of a carpet scrap, dip a cotton swab into it, and lay a spot at the point where you will begin setting new tufts or loops. The cement dries rapidly—apply it to one small area at a time, and avoid getting it on the carpet pile.

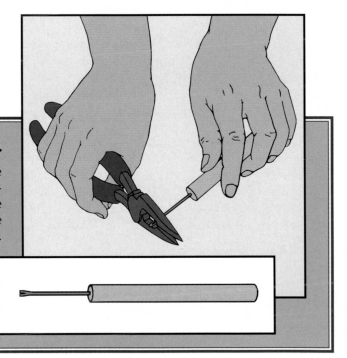

A TOOL FOR SETTING CARPET TUFTS

The makings of a tuft-setter consist of a large needle of the type used for sewing squares of knitting together and a $\frac{3}{8}$-inch wooden dowel. Cut a 4-inch length of dowel and drill a $\frac{1}{16}$-inch hole about 1 inch deep into one end. Insert the needle point into the hole and tap it with a hammer, driving the point into the wood. Using wire cutters or the cutting section of a pair of long-nose pliers *(right)*, clip most of the eye from the needle, leaving a shallow V-shaped end *(inset)*. To complete the tuft-setter, round and smooth this end with a small file or sharpening stone.

3. Replacing the pile.

◆ For cut-pile carpet, fold a tuft into a V over the tip of the tuft-setter and punch it into the latex-swabbed backing with one or two light taps of a hammer *(right)*.

◆ Repeat the process, setting the tufts close together and spreading more cement as needed. For best results, set the new pile so that it protrudes above surrounding fibers, and trim it flush with scissors.

◆ For loop-pile carpet *(inset)*, punch one end of a long piece of yarn into the backing with a tuft-setter, then form successive loops from the same piece and set the bottom of each loop.

◆ Check each loop to be sure it is the same height as the existing pile. Pull a short loop up with tweezers; punch a long one farther into the backing with the tuft-setter.

PATCHING A LARGE AREA

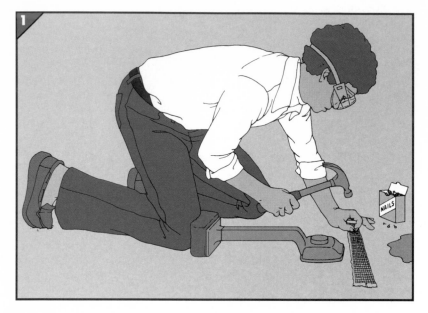

1. Stay-tacking.

◆ To reduce carpet tension for patching, set the teeth of a knee-kicker about a foot from the area to be patched and push the kicker forward. Be careful not to raise a hump in the carpet.

◆ Lay a strip of scrap carpet upside down just ahead of the knee-kicker and tack it to the floor with $1\frac{1}{2}$-inch nails at 3- to 4-inch intervals. Later, this strip of scrap carpet simplifies pulling out the nails without damaging the carpet.

◆ Release the knee-kicker and repeat the process on the other three sides of the damage.

2. Cutting a patch.

◆ From scrap carpet, measure out a patch slightly larger than the damaged area.

◆ Open a pathway through the pile with a blunt tool, such as a Phillips screwdriver, then pull the pile away from the cutting line with your fingers as you cut.

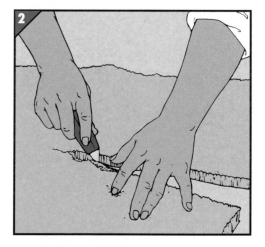

A COOKIE CUTTER FOR SMALL REPAIRS

If the damaged area is less than 4 inches in diameter, rent a tool like that at left, which cuts both a hole in the carpet and a patch to fit, consolidating Steps 2, 3, and 4.

Four spikes penetrate the backing to hold the tool in place as you twist it to work the sharp, serrated edge through. Do not cut the underlying carpet pad except with cushion-back carpet *(page 125)*. Use the same technique to cut a matching patch, then glue it in place as explained in Step 6 on page 124.

3. Cutting a hole.

◆ Place the patch over the damaged area, matching pattern and pile direction.
◆ With one edge of the patch acting as a guide, cut through the carpet and backing to a point about $\frac{1}{2}$ inch from each edge of the patch. Open a pathway for the knife between rows of pile as you cut. Do not cut the pad beneath the carpet.
◆ Lift the patch and cut completely around the damaged area to create a hole about $\frac{1}{2}$ inch smaller than the patch on three sides, as shown by the light gray lines in the illustration *(right)*.

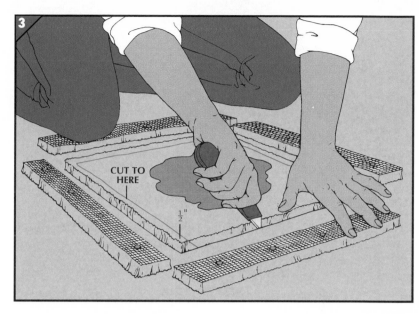

4. Trimming the hole.

◆ Position the patch to overlap the hole evenly on three sides, and stay-tack the edge used in Step 3 as a guide for the first carpet cut *(left)*.
◆ Cut around the anchored patch to enlarge the hole in the carpet to fit snugly around all sides of the patch.
◆ Pull the nails used to secure the patch and remove it from the hole.

5. Placing seam tape.

◆ Cut four strips of seam tape about an inch longer than the sides of the hole, and spread each strip with a thin layer of latex seam adhesive—just enough to fill in the weave of the tape.
◆ Slip each strip beneath an edge of the hole so that the cut edge of the carpet lies on the centerline.
◆ Squeeze a thin bead of adhesive along the edges of the carpet backing; avoid getting any adhesive on the pile.

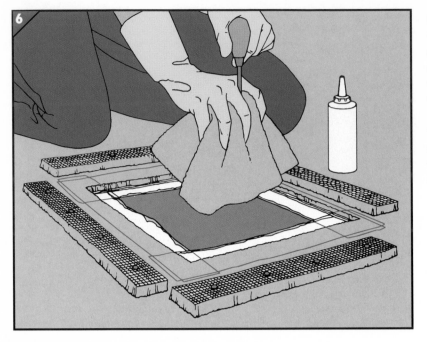

6. Putting in the patch.

◆ Cup the patch in your hand if it is small enough. Otherwise, push an awl through the center of the patch, then fold the patch downward into a tent shape *(left)*.

◆ Position the patch over the hole, and push it off the awl. As the edges of the patch move toward the sides of the hole, they will pick up small amounts of adhesive from the tape.

◆ Push the edges of patch and carpet together and press on the seam around the patch with the heel of your hand. With the awl, free tufts or loops of pile crushed into the seam, and brush your fingers back and forth across the seam to blend the pile of carpet and patch.

◆ After about 5 hours, tug the carpet scraps to remove nails from around the patch, and restore the overall tension on the carpet by using the knee-kicker opposite the patch at all four walls of the room.

MENDING A SURFACE RIP

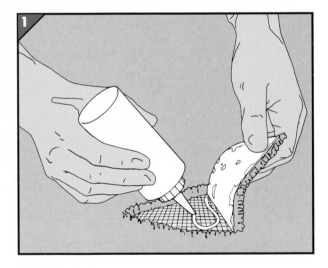

1. Sealing the flap.

◆ If the backing is undamaged, lift the torn section of carpet pile and clean out any loose pile or dried cement.

◆ Apply latex seam adhesive to the exposed backing *(left)*, then spread it in a thin coating over the backing.

2. Hiding the seam.

◆ Press the ripped pile against the adhesive and hold it in place with one hand while you rub the carpet surface with a smooth object, such as the bottom of a glass bottle *(right)*. Rub firmly from the rip toward the sound carpet to work the adhesive into the backing. If any adhesive oozes to the surface, clean it off immediately with water and detergent.

◆ After 4 or 5 hours, when the adhesive has dried, replace any pile that is missing *(page 121)*.

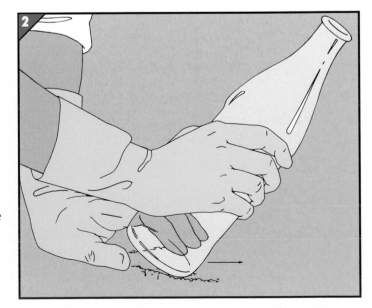

REPAIRS FOR CUSHION-BACK CARPET

1. Applying floor adhesive.

◆ After cutting out the damaged area and a patch to fit, scrape any dried cement from the floor with a sharpened putty knife.

◆ Spread multipurpose flooring adhesive on the clean floor using a $\frac{3}{32}$-inch notched trowel. Press firmly on the trowel to leave a pattern of adhesive ridges separated by bare floor.

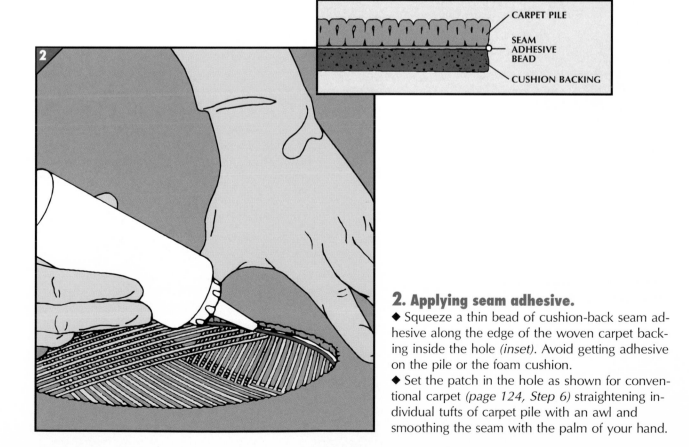

CARPET PILE

SEAM ADHESIVE BEAD

CUSHION BACKING

2. Applying seam adhesive.

◆ Squeeze a thin bead of cushion-back seam adhesive along the edge of the woven carpet backing inside the hole *(inset)*. Avoid getting adhesive on the pile or the foam cushion.

◆ Set the patch in the hole as shown for conventional carpet *(page 124, Step 6)* straightening individual tufts of carpet pile with an awl and smoothing the seam with the palm of your hand.

INDEX

Time-Life Books is a division of Time Life Inc.

PRESIDENT and CEO: John M. Fahey Jr.
EDITOR-IN-CHIEF: John L. Papanek

TIME-LIFE BOOKS

MANAGING EDITOR: Roberta Conlan

Director of Design: Michael Hentges
Director of Editorial Operations:
  Ellen Robling
Director of Photography and Research:
  John Conrad Weiser
Senior Editors: Russell B. Adams Jr.,
  Dale M. Brown, Janet Cave, Lee Hassig,
  Robert Somerville, Henry Woodhead
Special Projects Editor: Rita Thievon
  Mullin
Director of Technology: Eileen Bradley
Library: Louise D. Forstall

PRESIDENT: John D. Hall

Vice President, Director of Marketing:
  Nancy K. Jones
Vice President, Director of New Product
  Development: Neil Kagan
Vice President, Book Production: Marjann
  Caldwell
Production Manager: Marlene Zack
Quality Assurance Manager: James King

HOME REPAIR AND IMPROVEMENT

SERIES EDITOR: Lee Hassig
Administrative Editor: Barbara Levitt

Editorial Staff for Floors and Stairways
Art Directors: Kathleen Mallow,
  David Neal Wiseman
Picture Editor: Catherine Chase Tyson
Text Editor: James Michael Lynch
Associate Editors/Research-Writing:
  Dan Kulpinski, Terrell Smith
Technical Art Assistant: Angela Miner
Senior Copyeditor: Juli Duncan
Copyeditor: Judith Klein
Picture Coordinator: Paige Henke
Editorial Assistant: Amy S. Crutchfield

Special Contributors: John Drummond
  (illustration); William Graves, Craig
  Hower, Marvin Shultz, Eileen Wentland
  (digital illustration); George Constable,
  Brian McGinn (text); Mel Ingber (index);
  Catherine Hackett (picture research).

Correspondents: Christine Hinze (London),
  Christina Lieberman (New York), Maria
  Vincenza Aloisi (Paris).

PICTURE CREDITS

Cover: Photograph, Michael Latil; Art,
  Carol Hilliard, Totally Incorporated.

Illustrators: W. Hollis Anderson, George
  Bell, Frederic F. Bigio from B-C Graph-
  ics, Roger C. Essley, Gerry Gallagher,
  Great, Inc., Walter Hilmers Jr., Fred
  Holz, Gérard Mariscalchi, John Massey,
  Peter McGinn, Joan S. McGurren,
  Jacques Proulx, Nicholas Schrenk, Ray
  Skibinski, Vantage Art, Inc., Vicki Vebell,
  Whitman Studio, Inc.

Photographers: **End papers:** Michael Latil
  (front); Renée Comet (back). 7: Clarke
  Industries, Inc. 9: Michael Latil. 18:
  Porter-Cable Power Tools. 22, 26:
  Michael Latil. 28: Clarke Industries,
  Inc. 31: Michael Latil. 41: Courtesy
  of Senco Products, Inc. 44, 47, 61, 63:
  Michael Latil. 71: Renée Comet. 76:
  Michael Latil. 77: Trus Joist MacMillan.
  87: Michael Latil. 94, 101: Renée
  Comet. 102: Michael Latil. 109: Renée
  Comet. 112: Roberts Consolidated In-
  dustries, Inc. 122: Michael Latil.

ACKNOWLEDGMENTS

Crescencio Batalla, Trussway, Inc., Freder-
icksburg, Va.; Bill Cochran, Home Depot,
Alexandria, Va.; Mike Dawson, A & A
Rental, Alexandria, Va.; Kirk Grundahl,
Wood Truss Council of America, Madison,
Wis.; Kevin and Kate Hardardt, Alexandria,
Va.; Glen Hasenyager, Trus Joist MacMil-
lan, Boise, Idaho; Uel Johnson, Prince
Georges County Office of Central Services,
Forestville, Md.; Jim Keener, J&J Industries,
Dalton, Ga.; Susan Levine, Prescott Healy
Co., Ltd., Chicago; Mac Mackay, The Rug
Man, Alexandria, Va.; Timothy K. McCool,
National Wood Flooring Association, Man-
chester, Mo.; Bill Price Jr., Preferred Prod-
ucts, Inc., Seattle; Glen Robak, Trus Joist
MacMillan, Boise, Idaho; Judy Rodde,
Roberts Consolidated Industries, Inc., City
of Industry, Calif.; Biff Roberts, Senco
Products, Inc., Cincinnati; Richard C.
Robertson, Covey's Carpet and Drapes,
Springfield, Va.; Bob Snitzer, Century Stair
Company, Haymarket, Va.; Leopoldo Soto,
Trussway, Inc., Fredericksburg, Va.; Gary
Sweatt, Trussway, Inc., Hurst, Tex.; Jim
Thomas, Trussway, Inc., Fredericksburg,
Va.; Carroll Turner, The Carpet and Rug
Institute, Dalton, Ga.

First printing. Printed in U.S.A.
Published simultaneously in Canada.
School and library distribution by Time-Life
Education, P.O. Box 85026, Richmond,
Virginia 23285-5026.

TIME-LIFE is a trademark of Time Warner
Inc. U.S.A.

**Library of Congress
Cataloging-in-Publication Data**
Floors and stairways / by the editors of
  Time-Life Books.
p. cm. — (Home repair and improve-
  ment)
Includes index.
ISBN 0-7835-3887-1
1. Floors—Maintenance and repair—Ama-
  teurs' manuals. 2. Staircases—Mainte-
  nance and repair—Amateurs' manuals.
I. Time-Life Books. II. Series.
TH2528.F577   1995
694—dc20   95-8607